THE GIRL NEXT DOOR MEETS CANCER

Love Always and Forever,
Hayles xoxo

BY HAYLEIGH O'BRIEN
DECEMBER 12, 1985-DECEMBER 16, 2017

FriesenPress

Suite 300 - 990 Fort St
Victoria, BC, V8V 3K2
Canada

www.friesenpress.com

ISBN
978-1-5255-4432-3 (Hardcover)
978-1-5255-4433-0 (Paperback)
978-1-5255-4434-7 (eBook)

1. BIOGRAPHY & AUTOBIOGRAPHY, PERSONAL MEMOIRS

Distributed to the trade by The Ingram Book Company

This read will captivate you, and pull on all of your emotions from laughter, anger and tears. Hayleigh was what many people strive to be in life; confident, honest, loving, pure, raw, straight to the point, someone you wanted around. Hayleigh was motivating, genuine and told you how it was; someone who knew what mattered most. Life can throw you curve balls and Hayleigh knew this, but through her journey she teaches us through her lived experiences there is one thing we need to remember, no matter what there is always hope.

—Kate Magee, Supervisor, MHSU Services

Honest, gut-wrenching read as we know now how it ended. Makes her more amazing to have persevered through all the unexpected decisions she was given. She faced each one timely, with humour and rich vocabulary, nothing left undone. After reading I moved on my decades old postponed decisions and attacked a resentful and unforgiving spirit I had towards my family and friends. Thank you Hayleigh Noel.

—Wanda T., Registered Nurse

Hayleigh Connell O'Brien was no ordinary girl next door. As her blog reveals, she had old soul wisdom that kept her centered while experiencing the vulnerability and heartbreak of a young woman suddenly facing the loss of her deepest held hopes and dreams.

Hayleigh's last acts were particularly courageous. By allowing us to know intimate details of her with journey with a rare and aggressive cancer she provides patients, families and professionals alike unique awareness of what it can be like to face one's worst fears. She also helps us to understand what is sustaining, and what truly matters in the end.

—Lyn MacBeath, MD

"She stood in the storm, and when the wind did not blow her way, she adjusted her sails."

—*Unknown*

FORWARD

On a clear, crisp morning in September of 2017, Hayleigh and I started out on what we hoped would be a daily ritual for many years to come. In an attempt to pursue our goal of living healthy, at 8:00 each morning, we began our daily three-mile walk around our small community. This was to be a five-day weekly routine. It was a ritual of hope for both of us.

As we walked, the conversation began with feathers.

"Did you know that black feathers are good—they mean you are being protected! White feathers mean you are surrounded by angels; black and white feathers mean change is coming," Hayleigh told me.

Along the way, we searched for feathers, and after finding several black and white ones along our route, we both said that if change was in fact coming, we hoped it would be good!

During this particular walk, the conversation progressed from feathers to wedding plans (December 25 was the day her and Keith had chosen, as all our family—including those from PEI—would be there), to Christmas, to Hayleigh's Blog.

"Last night, I was talking to Tim and Gail," Hayleigh said. "Tim feels that I need to publish my blog, and that it should be used as a resource for patients facing the cancer battle, and as a teaching tool for residents who are working with cancer patients. Tim says it has some good insights that will help new doctors see the way real patients feel, especially given the way a resident might respond. If they know what they say can cause issues, maybe hearing this from someone going through the battle will help them understand. When I'm feeling better, I think that's what I will do … publish my blog."

Of course, as her very proud momma, I told her that I thought this was a great idea! I had been following the blog, and I thought it would be a good resource for anyone dealing with any life-threatening disease.

As we continued our walk, the conversation turned dark.

"Mom," she said, "if I die, will you make sure that my blog gets published?"

"Of course, I will, but like I keep telling you, dying is not in my vocabulary. When you get better, you and I will look into publishing the blog, and we will make sure that it is used to help others …"

In October of 2016, our daughter, Hayleigh, was diagnosed with a very rare large cell neuroendocrine tumour (LCNET) combined with an ovarian adenocarcinoma. At that time, we were told there had been approximately thirty documented cases of this type of disease.[1] Hayleigh underwent two rounds of chemo (the first round was completed, and the second round was only given for two or three days and then stopped, as it was not doing what the doctors had hoped it would.

---

[1] *In February 2018, I talked with Dr. Aubertine from BCCA. Dr. Aubertine said that indeed this cancer was rare—so rare that there were no other reported cases. The thirty cases cited initially, when Hayleigh had first been diagnosed, were similar, but not the same. We were also informed during that consult that of the seventy markers they used in genetic testing, none of them came back positive. This cancer was not familial (we had several family members, including Hayleigh's dad and sister, diagnosed with cancer): it was environmental.

After her diagnosis, Hayleigh began looking at her life and all the things she hoped it would hold. The following is her "bucket list":

- *Marry Keith*
- *Get a puppy*
- *Ireland*
- *Big birthday celebration*
- *Christmas*
- *PEI*
- *Watch a sunset*
- *Watch a sunrise*

In some ways, she was able to accomplish a few of these plans: PEI, watch a sunset, watch a sunrise, have a birthday celebration (December 12 was her 32 birthday).

Sadly, her upcoming marriage to Keith was not to be realized (December 25, 2017), nor was her favourite holiday: Christmas.

Because of this, we have chosen to honour her wish to marry Keith and have published this book under the name "Hayleigh O'Brien."

Hayleigh was awaiting a third trial of chemo when, on December 16, 2017, she suddenly passed away at the local hospice while out walking her beloved dog.

This is her journey, in her own words.

The Beginning...I Think...
How this whole journey began...
October 6, 2016

It's been a whirlwind of a few days. I have been feeling unwell for the past few weeks and things culminated on Monday. Before I get to that, I should explain what led to this "culmination."

A little over a month ago, I noticed a hardness in my lower abdomen, but only when I was lying down. I didn't feel any pain, but that, combined with peeing a lot (not unusual for me—you can ask anyone who knows me) and being exhausted, had me worried. I had a nursing friend do a urine screen on me (this is what good friends do for you, by the way) to check for a urinary tract infection (UTI) and it came back negative. Then I gave myself a pregnancy test (three to be honest), and when those all came back negative, I tried to push it from my mind and was successful with that until late September.

I went to hot yoga with my mom one night and found that even though I am out of shape, I couldn't do a forward fold, I couldn't lie on my back or stomach comfortably, and I was unable to do more than half the poses. I got up the courage to ask my mom to press my stomach—I think the "no speaking" rule of hot yoga gave me the confidence boost, since I don't think I was ready to hear that it was bad. With an alarmed look in her eyes, she whispered, "You need to see the doctor." From this point on, things moved at a relatively quick pace—both internally with whatever was going on, and in my life. The next Monday, I called the doctor, and I was given an appointment for three weeks: the soonest available.

I continued on with life, and around the last week of September, I felt more fatigued and the nausea started to settle in. I was missing half days and full days of work, and my entire abdomen had started to harden. I tried to figure out what could be wrong, and in a world of Google I had narrowed it down to irritable bowl (which I figured was manageable), lactose intolerance (I could give up dairy, except for cheese and ice cream, but I figured the suffering was worth those two), ovarian cancer (too young and no family history) and ovarian cyst (these are common, so it's a good chance). People started to notice that I didn't look well and encouraged me to take care of myself. In hindsight, I've had a few people comment that I had gained a noticeable amount of weight, but they didn't want to offend me. I called the doctor's office and asked for an earlier appointment if anyone cancelled, and was told they'd call me if this was available. They never called, so I lived on ginger ale, crackers, and Gravol and stayed home and rested as much as I could.

On October 3, 2016, I attended my doctor's appointment at 11:30 a.m. as scheduled. I was nervous, but I was also feeling so terrible that I was just hopeful he would know what was wrong. My family and friends had been encouraging: "It's just the flu," "it's stress," etc.... but I was ready to find out exactly how well I had diagnosed myself with the internet. I should note that I hate going to the doctor—not that he isn't a nice man, but I always feel that I am wasting his time and feel guilty. This partly played a role in my waiting so long after discovering the hardness before seeing the doctor. If not for the validation from my mom that I needed to see him, I probably would not have made the appointment even at that point.

As I talked to him, I began to tear up, and it all fell out of my mouth rather clumsily. I explained, "I'm not feeling well, I am tired all the time, I've gained fifteen pounds in the past two to three months, and I know I'm not the healthiest person, but I haven't changed things enough to gain that much, and I am peeing all the time—well, more than usual, and ... there is a hardness in my abdomen ..." While he seems like a lovely man, he looked at me in a way that I perceived as scepticism, and he asked me to lie down on the bed. I did as asked, and he started to push on my stomach. He felt around for a while. I tried to look anywhere but at him, when I did, he had a look of surprise on his face, and he said, "I'll be right back." This is the moment I started to be really worried. I'd never had a doctor leave me in the room, but then again, I don't visit that often, if I can help it. He returned and stood at the end of the bed and asked, "Are you sure you're not pregnant?"

I answered in probably an exasperated tone, "No, I don't see how I could be, I take my birth control every day at 7:25 a.m., and I have taken three tests and they were all negative."

He responded, "Well, your uterus feels about thirty-six weeks pregnant."

At this statement, I almost had a heart attack. He again asked to leave the room, and while he was gone, I frantically looked at the calendar at my phone. I had started dating my boyfriend at the beginning of January, so this would be a shock to both of us. All I could think of was, "thirty-six weeks, that's a baby, like a full-sized, can-come-out-and-survive baby ..." We had discussed having children, but this was definitely not in the plans for either of us. In retrospect, I would have taken the baby.

The doctor returned and asked if he could do an ultrasound. Of course, I said yes, but as we both listened to the handheld machine there was no heartbeat—there was only the gurgling sounds of my stomach. I can't remember if I was relieved or not. He put the machine down and said that he would like me to go to the hospital that day to have a formal ultrasound and that he would arrange it with the hospital before I left. He said what I appreciated to be an honest and comforting thing, which was, "I'm not sure what's wrong with you, but something is not right in there," and he gestured to my abdomen. Why I needed this validation, I am not sure, but it was reassuring, and after doing one last pregnancy test (it was negative), I went to meet my mom for lunch.

By 1:30 that afternoon, only two hours after my appointment, I was up at the hospital and waiting for an ultrasound. I drank my requisite water and listened to the pregnant women in the room complain about having to pee. My name was called, and I changed into my gown and lay down on the table. For the next thirty minutes, the ultrasound tech dug around in my abdomen looking for whatever it was that was happening. Once she was done, she asked me to get dressed and told me that she would speak with the radiologist and I should be able to leave. I was in the midst of reassuring my mother and boyfriend that things were all good and I would be headed home soon.

The technician returned less than ten minutes later and said, "The radiologist has spoken to your family doctor, and they want you to have a CT scan."

My level of anxiety went up yet again, as my first thought was, *This must be bad, if the doctor and radiologist have already spoken—they are worried too.* I work in health care, and to try and connect with any doctor is time-consuming, so for that to happen so quickly, I was concerned.

I let my mom know where I was headed, and she immediately said, "I'm getting your dad and we will be there right away." I tried to reassure her and tell her not to bother, and that I would be done shortly, but I think her mom-sense knew better.

I went through the CT scan—just one of the many medical experiences to come—and while waiting for someone to tell me what the hell was happening, my parents arrived. Shortly after that, we were directed to the emergency room (ER) to see another doctor. In my mad need to control things, I Googled the doctor, because I still had no idea what was wrong, and I thought that maybe if I knew what kind of doctor she or he was, I would be able to figure it out. She, as it turned out, was/is an obstetrician/gynaecologist. Well, that narrowed my diagnoses down to the cyst or the cancer, and neither was particularly comforting. As I sat in the designated gyne room in the ER waiting for the doctor, I wasn't sure what I was feeling or thinking, but I know that my mind was racing.

The specialist showed up, and while she looked about fifteen years old, she was reassuring and pleasant, and she told me that there was a mass on my left ovary and it was large; according to the CT report it was about 22.8 centimeters, and it was likely an ovarian cystadenoma or cystadenocarcinoma. This was the "culmination" of all the symptoms, and the self-doubt, and the need for validation from the medical system. The doctor did an exam—one of the first of uncomfortable exams that women have to endure in these situations. My parents and my boyfriend (who had been informed by a friend that I was still in the hospital) were with me as the doctor explained that I would need surgery to determine what exactly the mass was. She said that she had been in contact with the BC Cancer Agency (BCCA). This was the first mention of cancer, and given a childhood experience of my dad having had cancer, it surprisingly did not alarm me. I sat stoically and listened to her say that I would need surgery, and that it could be done at home where they would remove the mass and do pathology and determine what it is, or I could wait and have the surgery in Vancouver at the BCCA. She said that it was possible for them to do the pathology while I am under anaesthetic and I could possibly end up having a complete hysterectomy if they find cancer. This was the first moment that I lost it. I had never been completely sure that I wanted children, but with my boyfriend I was more inclined and had imagined how cute our future children would be (for the record, they'd be really cute), but the moment she said I may have to have a hysterectomy it was too much. I saw the look on my parents' face, and I saw the dream of my adorable future children go up in smoke, and it was more than I could handle, but I managed to pull myself together and decided to have the surgery here at home and go from there.

This was the beginning of my journey, though I am not sure when the mass actually started growing. This is when I had to start making decisions for my life that no one plans to make. While writing this blog came from a conversation with family and friends, I hope that my experience can encourage other women to pay attention to their bodies and trust their instincts. While I needed validation of what I "knew" was wrong with my body, I hope my journey can give someone encouragement and maybe direction to pay attention, ask questions, and not be afraid to talk to their doctor.

Surgery scheduled

October 12, 2016

I saw the ob-gyn today in follow-up from the hospital. Mom, Dad, and Keith came with me. The surgery is scheduled for the 27th of October. I'm disappointed that it's so far away, but the other part of me says that if it were more serious they would get me in sooner. The doctor said that the blood work looks good. The CA-125, which they typically look at for ovarian cancer, was normal. Only the CA-19 was elevated, but she said that it isn't anything to be concerned about, as it is most likely due to inflammation from the mass. I'm anxious about the surgery, but at the same time I'm ready for it to come out. I feel like this thing—or "Felicia," as we have taken to calling it—has grown. I could just be paranoid, or just more aware of it.

Feeling shitty, but now with pain

October 25, 2016

It's been a really long few weeks. Being home is not quite the same when you feel shitty. A couple nights ago I started to have a really sharp and achy pain in my right side (not where "Felicia" currently resides). I hardly slept that night due to the pain waking me up. This is the first time I've had any pain at all, so I was worried that it might have ruptured or something medically gross like that. I would have gone to the ER in the middle of the night, but I knew that Keith would have wanted to go with me, and with his new job he needs his sleep. I waited until the next day and called the specialists office, and they said if I was concerned that I should go to the ER. I had my mom take me and ended up being there from 10:30 a.m. until around 6:00 p.m. yesterday. They did another ultrasound and confirmed what I had suspected. The mass has grown. "Felicia" has grown to 24 cm craniocaudal by 13 cm AP by 27 cm trans. I'm not sure what all that means, but it's big. Not only can I feel it, but the staff at the hospital seemed both intrigued yet horrified. I had a resident doctor do an exam and ask if she could feel it, because she had "never felt anything that big inside someone, so it'd be good learning" for her. Not one to impede any learning, I let her have a go. I honestly look eight to nine months pregnant, and if this is what pregnancy feels like, I don't know why people do it more than once. They gave me pain medications to try and manage the pain and nausea until surgery and offered for me to stay in the hospital until the 27th. I'd rather be at home and at least trying to manage it with the medications. I hardly eat, and I am no longer comfortable in any position. My fear of surgery is quickly being outweighed by the needs to get this thing out!

Bye, Felicia!

November 4, 2016

I am tumour-free. The surgery went very well. It was a long few days, but I'm on the mend. Keith, Mom, Dad, and I arrived at the hospital at 6:00 a.m. on the 7th and were sent to day surgery. I was called to the back and changed into the gown. They took some blood, which the technician missed on the first try. I took this as a bad omen, but "Felicia" needed to go, so I maintained my calm for about two minutes before the woman who was coming to put the IV in my hand arrived and the tears flowed freely. This is the second time this journey I have really cried. The shot of heparin before didn't help either; if you've ever had it, you know what I mean. They let my mom come back. It's amazing how at thirty years old I still need my mom. My dad and boyfriend came back, and I said good-bye to them. My mom and Keith went to work, and my dad was there as the nurse came and put my hair hat on, and she and the ob-gyn wheeled me down to the surgical hallway. My dad kissed me good-bye, carrying my purse on his shoulder and said he'd see me soon.

I pulled it together until we arrived in the surgical theatre, and then the tears started flowing. I remember asking the surgeon for a picture of the mass, mostly out of my abnormal sense of curiosity. I had the most amazing nurse. I cannot tell you her name, and I couldn't accurately pick her out in a line-up, but I can tell you she was so compassionate and comforting. She reassured me and wiped my tears as I cried. "I don't know what to expect," I said—the fear of the unknown. The last thing I remember was a male doctor saying, "Hayleigh, I'm going to give you something to slee ..."

The next thing I knew, I woke up in the recovery room and felt nothing. I managed to come to, and I asked the nurse first for some water, and secondly, for some strange reason, "Do I still have an appendix?" Of all the things to ask, I realize this is strange, but I knew going in they might take it, and for some reason my brain perceived this as the most pressing issue. The ob-gyn came in to talk to me and showed me the picture of "Felicia." She was somehow bigger than I had expected. My initial thought was that she looked like a fat liver, all smooth and bruised-looking. She told me that the mass was actually bigger than that, as they had to drain another 1.5L just to remove it. I was oddly proud, but also disgusted that my body had grown this ... thing! She said that the pathologist would be looking at it, but that it was likely that I would need more surgery, as the mass apparently looked "malignant." I don't think this truly settled in my head, as I was still a bit out of it, but it was a conversation that haunts me a little.

They gave me a popsicle and wheeled me over to the women's ward where I found my dad waiting patiently. He followed us into the private room I was set up in, and I immediately told him to turn on my phone. He questioned my senses, wondering why on earth I needed to text at this time, but when he saw the picture of "Felicia" he sat stunned. It was the first of many stunned faces to see the mass, in all her glory. I felt oddly protective of her, while also being disgusted by her.

I spent the next three days in the hospital, luckily with plenty of visitors. I am very blessed to have an amazing support system, including my incredible parents, who showed up every day, and my amazing boyfriend, who stayed with me until I had to sleep, and my family and friends, who visited regularly and texted me to keep me company. Visitors help, and I felt a bit guilty once I was moved into a four-bed room, given my bed area always had visitors, but I was so grateful for the love and support. People sent me gorgeous flowers that brightened my day, and my coworkers sent me a huge gift basket to keep my mind busy.

Coming home was nice, and I relished the idea of a shower. Keith has set up our bedroom to accommodate my recovery, bringing the TV and DVD player upstairs and a mini fridge with snacks for me. It's a perfect set-up. Mom spent the day with me, and we chatted, and napped, and watched movies. I am not good at not doing anything, but I want to heal up so I can get back to real life, go back to work, and carry on.

Last night, lying in bed, everything hit me. I don't think I have cried that hard since all of this started. I couldn't stop myself—it was as if every fear, every piece of me turned to tears. Luckily, Keith was there to hold me together.

I had my follow-up with the surgeon today. I'm not ready to write about it yet, so I'll hold off.

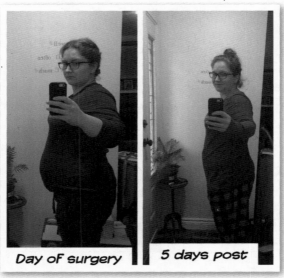

Hayles Pre and Post surgery

LIFE PROCESSED, KIND OF

NOVEMBER 6, 2016

I've had a couple days to process things, and I still don't feel like they've sunken in. Mom, Keith, and I met with the ob-gyn on Friday at 9:00 a.m. She's been an amazing doctor; however, her poker face could use some work. When she walked out, into the waiting area, and saw us, there was a look of pity on her face, and I knew it was not good news. We sat in the exam room waiting, and it's funny, but while I remember most of the conversation, I felt like my brain went numb. She said that the mass was a combination of "benign," "low malignancy," and "high malignancy" areas. She said that it was "cancer," and that the pathologist in Kamloops had sent the mass to the BC Cancer Agency to be reviewed. The good news in all of this is that the biopsy of the omentum (the layer of fat that covers your organs) was negative for cancer, as was my appendix and the free fluid in my abdomen. She informed us that she would be referring me to the BCCA. We were told there would be treatment options, and a few listed included more surgery (including the dreaded and emotionally charged hysterectomy), chemotherapy and/or radiation, and in the best-case scenario, they would just monitor me until I had children, if we chose to do so, and then do more aggressive treatment like the hysterectomy in the future. And now, the dreaded waiting. I am a planner by nature, and it's literally my day job to help problem solve and organize people's lives, and I cannot do that for myself because I don't have enough information.

I feel a bit lost. I mean, I had cancer? Is there more? Could it come back? What should I be doing? I don't know what any of it means, and I don't know what to do or what to feel. I'm scared and confused and going through the motions feels like a bit of a life raft, but it's like this nagging thing at the back of my mind asking me things I don't know the answers to. It's overwhelming, and yet like my brain is running on autopilot. I guess I'd let autopilot brain run until we heard from BC Cancer.

Urge to Google

Another great weekend. It was low key, but it as spent with Keith, which makes it great. I found myself obsessing about the results of my cancer. I still haven't heard about my appointment, and in not knowing, I become almost frantic for information. This usually results in Googling any information I can. It always comes to a dead end, and since I don't have enough detail, I find it makes me more frantic, but it also makes me feel like I have some semblance of control, no matter how false it might be. My supports keep telling me to not search for information, but honestly, sometimes it feels like a compulsion that I can't control.

A LONG DAY

NOVEMBER 23, 2016

Grandma Yvonne passed away today. It's been a long day, but in the end, she is no longer suffering. It also happens to be the day that I got the call from BC Cancer. I go down there next week on Tuesday November 29, 2016, at 8:00 a.m. I feel better knowing, but now it's about the plan.

Grandma Yvonne

Duck feet

November 28, 2016

I feel like a duck: like I'm calm on the surface, but I feel completely frantic under the surface. There is this chaotic energy in my body that I cannot seem to shake. I can't focus on anything. I feel like there are these unknown entities are making life decisions for me, and I have no idea what is going on! I feel like I can't trust my body, because who the hell knows what is going on with it. I want this to be over.

I think I'm feel agitated even more right now since BC Cancer called and want me to stay longer to do a PET Scan. I'm so frustrated. We are about to leave for Vancouver, and now I'm trying to deal with this. I feel like I'm going to explode!

Now we know...

November 29, 2016

It's been another long day, following all the other long days I've had lately. We arrived in Vancouver last night safe and sound around 9:15 p.m. and settled in to the hotel after the 3+ hour drive on the Coquihalla—a road I hate driving on in the wintery months. We are only a couple blocks from the BCCA, so we can walk there in the morning. We got up this morning and got ready. Keith and Dad ate breakfast, I didn't want to eat in case they could squeeze a PET scan in, and we headed over to BCCA. It was a short five-minute walk. I filled out paperwork, and then we went up to the second floor. We met with a nurse who took my vitals, etc.... and then we did a personal history with one of the doctors.

This doctor asked me, "What do you know?"

And for whatever reason, I said everything except cancer. I'm not sure why I couldn't bring myself to say it, but she quickly made it clear that I had cancer. It was then that she dropped the "you have a rare type of cancer ... there are only about thirty documented cases." She still hadn't said what it was, but in my state of shock at this revelation, I didn't think to ask what it was called. I had to have yet another pelvic exam, and for this I sent my dad and Keith away to get some coffee. Once they were out of the room, I asked what it was called, and all I took in at that moment was "large," "cell," and "endocrine." It sounded, long, complicated, and scary. I survived the now-dreaded pelvic exam, and then she said she'd be back. In the time that it took her to leave, and for Dad and Keith to come back, I had already scrambled to my cell phone and searched those words and found out that the actual name was large cell neuroendocrine carcinoma, and I found the study that alluded to the thirty cases. I read a few lines and then shut it down before my dad and Keith walked in. I will admit that if I could do that moment over again, I would not have looked it up. It was nothing that I needed to read, and it certainly did not help to overcome my current state of shock.

A wonderful surprise of the morning was that one of my best friends showed up and waited with us until the original doctor and the medical oncologist arrived. I'm not sure the nursing staff was used to that much laughter coming from a room where people were just told that one of them has a rare form of cancer, but it's moments like that which made today not feel too scary or unbearable.

Hayles & Kristi Selfie

I had two types of cancer, the ovarian cystadenocarcinoma and the LCNEC of the ovary, in the original mass, a.k.a., "Felicia." They said that they are typically both aggressive, and that we needed to treat them just as aggressively. We were told that because this type is so rare that there are some unknowns in regard to treatment, and it will be treated like a small cell lung cancer, which is also aggressive. There was no plethora of options provided, just one: chemotherapy. I discussed my plan to go back to work next week, and the oncologist immediately said, "You're not going back to work on Monday, and probably not for a while."

I knew that things were going to move fairly quickly, but I did not expect the timeline of starting treatment next week. They explained that I would be given two types of chemotherapy: cis-platin and etoposide. The doctor went through side effects that I can expect to experience, all of which were not a surprise to me, having witnessed my dad go through chemotherapy almost twenty years ago. These included nausea and vomiting, diarrhea, mouth sores, and hair loss. I tried to not let my vanity get the best of me, but I admit that the hair loss brought tears to my eyes. I should explain that my hair is kind of my "thing"—not that I am entirely defined by my hair, but I have long, curly, and to be a bit narcis-sistic, awesome hair, which it took many years to truly appreciate. I like my big hair, but I also don't want the cancer to come back, so it's good-bye hair.

Hayles Big Hair

We discussed the things to look out for: fever, etc.... and while she said we shouldn't be too concerned with the "rare" side effects, in my mind, I thought given that I have this "rare" cancer, maybe we shouldn't discount the unlikely too quickly! She reviewed the importance of having great supports and taking people up on their offers to help, but also looking at the resources available through the cancer clinic and society in Kamloops.

The next big piece of the puzzle is around fertility. Given my emotional reaction to the word "hysterectomy" when all of this started, I feel surprisingly unconcerned about that. This doesn't mean I've changed my mind about having children, but I suppose I have unconsciously prioritized being healthy before that—if not, then I'm not sure if my brain has processed this. There was no talk of more surgery, which I'm grateful for. What we were told is that the chemo may have a mild to moderate risk of impacting my fertility, but they cannot say for sure what that impact might be. The doctors discussed referring me to a fertility clinic, and we agreed that this is a good plan just to have a better sense of our options. This makes me feel hopeful about my future, and the future that we might have as parents. And even if I cannot have my own children, there are other options for us to be parents, if that's what we decide, and we will travel that path if it comes to that.

After my relatively private outburst about the PET scan, my dad and Keith reassured me that they would rather have the PET scan done while we are here now, versus coming back on the weekend, and the clinic managed to schedule me for tomorrow morning. They also offered a referral for genetic counselling, noting that this may have consequences for my future children, and possibly my sister, my nephew, and any future nieces/nephews I may have. I agreed to the referral, and so we will for that to see what it means for the future.

We did some blood work before leaving, at which I am becoming a bit of a professional. Then, my dad, Keith, my friend, and I decided to eat and drink our feelings. We found a nearby pub and ate greasy and delicious food and we each had a drink, or two. And more importantly we laughed. I don't think I could have survived today without that laughter. This whole thing sucks, and I'm not trying to make light of it, but if you cannot laugh you are in trouble. I learned this in my work as a social worker, and dark humour is kind of a specialty in my family and friends.

We finished lunch and made our way back to the hotel to check back in. The financial strain of what is to come weighs heavily on me, and unfortunately is a reality for many people. I am extremely lucky to have the benefits and savings that I do, and a family that continues to offer their support in any way, including financially. My problem solver/practical tendencies took over, and I excused myself to go make the phone calls I had hoped to avoid by going back to work. I will run out of sick benefits (which, luckily, I have been on since October 3, 2016) on my birthday, in two weeks' time (happy birthday to me!—this is where my sarcasm comes out but doesn't quite translate to the written word). I will then go on employment insurance (55% of my usual wage) until I qualify for long-term disability (LTD) (70% of my usual wage) in February 2017. With the help of disability management, and union supports, I think I've figured out what I need to do and have gotten on top of all of that. I don't want to be a burden to anyone, especially not my parents, Keith, and my other family and friends who have already graciously offered financial support if needed. It will be a challenge, but historically I've not been one to run from a challenge.

For now, I am exhausted. Not physically, but mentally for sure. Emotionally, I'm not sure what I am, but I do know that it is a storm of emotions that will come to the surface eventually. Luckily, I have the support to help me weather anything cancer and chemotherapy can throw at me.

Angry bird

November 30, 2016

It's still all sinking in, but I'm still in practical mode, which means I got up at 4:00 a.m. (I couldn't sleep anymore), and then lay awake in bed for forty-five minutes before I snuck quietly to the bathroom to get ready while Dad and Keith slept. I got ready, sat quietly reading my e-reader in the dark, and then eventually went back to bed for another bit of sleep. We woke up, and this time headed straight to the BCCA. I wasn't allowed to eat anything before the scan but was directed to drink water.

We arrived the office, and I was taken into the back on my own. I changed into the standard hospital gown, and the technician put the port into my hand. I hate the needles into the hand, but I think I've gotten good at relaxing and letting it happen. The technician injected the radioactive stuff, and then I had to lie still for forty-five minutes. This was no easy task, and I truly think they should reconsider the process for this to not be after you've told someone they have cancer. Probably the last place that person should be is alone with their thoughts while radioactive material pumps through their body. But as with all things so far, I survived. We then headed to the PET scan machine, and this was a little bit more entertaining, but not much. This is where you lie on a hard table with your ankles in a foam holder, with a foam triangle under your knees, and your head in matching holder and, in an ever-so-uncomfortable way, hold your arms above your head for twenty minutes while you move back and forward through a giant mechanical donut. It was boring to say the least, but it's all done.

From there, we headed straight for breakfast! With a tummy full of breakfast, I said a teary good-bye to my friend who is off to travel the world and promised to talk regularly until we see one another soon. She made these last two days a little easier, and I am grateful for her presence, her energy, and mostly her support. It was from here that we made our way home and back to reality.

Reality feels a bit weird right now, but the storm of emotion started to surface. It always makes me laugh at how my emotional outpourings happen at strange times; tonight it was mid-dinner. Keith had made me a wonderful stir-fry, and for whatever reason I couldn't hold it in. I was angry—angry about all sorts of things, but mostly angry because I didn't do anything. And not that people who get cancer always get it for reasons, or because they do something, but I don't smoke, I hardly drink, and I have never done drugs (and I'm not just saying that because my parents are going to read this). I try and take care of my health, I like to walk and do yoga, and I'm angry that this is happening. I'm angry that the world continues to turn when it feels like it should have stopped. I'm angry at my body for betraying me, for growing the abomination that has led to all this. And being this angry makes me sad.

FEELING LOVED, AND FOR THAT I AM GRATEFUL

DECEMBER 1, 2016

I'm not sure what has gotten into me today, but I feel really good. I feel hopeful, and I feel energized. I know this may be fleeting, but I'm taking advantage of it to get this blog going. I actually feel good writing all of this out, and at this point if no one reads it, I'm okay with writing it if only for myself. I've always been a person who writes when they are stressed, never for other people to read, but I really would like to connect with other women who have experienced this, and I figure if they search "large cell neuroendocrine carcinoma of the ovary," they might be led here, and hopefully skip over the other stuff that Google provides. As I have said many times to the people in my life, "Don't Google it, trust me."

And even though those who could remember the name of it did Google it in spite of my warnings, I am still grateful for them, and for all of the supports in my life. As I have mentioned throughout, I have an amazing family, boyfriend, and friends, amazing colleagues, and even acquaintances and people I have never met who have reached out to offer their support. I have had offers of financial support, offers for transportation to chemotherapy, offers to chat and help process things, and I only found out two days ago. I have had people reach out just to say they are thinking of me and sending me prayers and positive energy, people I talk to regularly and people who I haven't spoken to in awhile, and I haven't even really posted anything on social media. I am equally grateful for all of their kind words and all of the good energy they send.

I haven't said it on here yet, but my parents in particular have been nothing short of incredible. They have been there through everything in my life, and have always gone above and beyond, and this experience has been nothing less than that. They show up, they are unwavering in their support, and they are the epitome of unconditional love. They have taken time from their jobs to be there for me, and for Keith, and I will never be able to thank them enough or repay them.

Hayles, Holly & Rick

I'm not sure where I was going with this post, but I feel the need to recognize how much I appreciate the supports I have, and how important they all are to me. They make life worth living, and they are my reasons to be.

Hair today, gone today

December 2, 2016

Today is the big day! I'm excited, but also really nervous. I've always had long hair, so I don't even know what to think. My mom and one of my best friends are coming to support me. I know that it'll be a bit of time before it will actually fall out, but I want to donate it; I don't want the chemo chemicals to prevent my hair from being able to do something good, so that's the reason for the pre-emptive haircut. That, and I feel like it gives me some sense of control in an out-of-control situation. Plus, my hair, when not in a messy mass on the top of my head, is actually a bit of work, whether it's curly or straight, and I don't think I'll have much energy for that. If all else fails, it's winter, and I have toques!

Hair Donation

CARRYING ON,
JUST WITH SHORT HAIR

DECEMBER 4, 2016

Well, I survived the haircut: part one the hair journey. I was not emotional at all—in fact, I think my hairdresser had a more difficult time than I did (she's known me "forever" and loves my hair). My mom and one of my best friends were there, and my dad was able to join us. Again, I'm extremely lucky, given that what I feared would be a sad and tearful moment was filled with laughter, love, and support. The feedback from friends, family, and supports has been very positive and reassuring. I actually kind of like it. I like to find silver linings, even though I like to think I'm more pessimistic/realistic than optimistic. And I suppose the silver lining in this is that I never would have ever cut my hair this short if not for the possibility of losing my hair, so I will find gratitude in that.

Last night we decorated our Christmas tree and it was normal. Life really has continued to move on, and that's a good thing. We had our shared traditions, and tried to create our own, it felt like peace on earth, and it again reassures me how blessed I am.

This morning I worked on my LTD paperwork. It is extremely frustrating and overwhelming. I feel for people without education or supports. I had a couple mini meltdowns, but Keith brought me back to earth. I got most of it done, so with his help and that of the employer supports I can get it all finished before I start chemo which is the goal.

Today I also picked up my meds for chemo, the ones they prescribe to help you manage the nausea and vomiting. It feels complicated, but as with anything on this journey, it's one step at a time.

It surprises me how much work and money goes with cancer. The paperwork, the organizing, and the cost. I'm lucky to have my medications 50% covered by my work benefits, but even then, it is still a surprising expense that I never would have guessed. This is the reality for people dealing with cancer?! It seems ludicrous to me.

I went for a visit with my aunt, uncle, and cousin, and we chatted about things of all sorts. They are huge supports for me, so it was nice to visit and chat and just spend time in their presence.

I also went to the dentist today. I luckily had this appointment from a few months ago, when all this started. They talked about some of the impact the chemo can have on the mouth. I knew from my dad's experience what can happen, but it's a good reminder. I'm glad I went and will do my best to pay attention to all aspects of my health, including dental health.

Anyways, as you can see, it's been a busy day, so I'm going to enjoy the rest of the weekend. Until later!

FEAR AND TEARS— IT'S "NORMAL," I THINK

DECEMBER 5, 2016

Overall, it's been an okay day emotionally, but a great day of relaxation and spending time with my parents and Keith.

I had a rough moment last night after I had written my post. I'm not sure where it came from, but I felt truly scared for the first time since this all started. I had a storm of a breakdown. I'm assuming those thoughts and fears are commonplace amongst people diagnosed, as well as the people in their lives, but I felt like I couldn't stop them. It was a vicious cycle, and trying to slow my brain down felt impossible. Again, Keith was there, and he reassured me. It was like I needed him to repeat all of the things the oncologists had said: "this is preventative (in regard to chemo)," "the PET scan was negative," "think of this as short-term pain for long-term gain," "we are going for cure, not just treatment." I needed someone else to say it, because saying it in my own head wasn't enough.

It scares me how quick the emotion comes on, and I never realized how tiring it can be trying to manage it. I feel super tired today, and then my head goes to, "maybe it's back, you were tired when it was in your body," and down a spiral of doubt I go. But then I remind myself that the test was negative, and if it hadn't grown elsewhere in the past month, it's not likely to sprout up in four days. With practicing some mindfulness, I noticed the feeling of anxiety and tears in my chest and throat and realized that I have been trying not to let any tears out today. I think I'm afraid that if I start I won't stop, and that it'll make the people around me upset. I know it's good to let it out, and that home is my safe place for that. It's just tiring. I've read the pamphlets about the emotional toll. I am lucky that there are resources out there, and while my initial thought was that I don't need any "formal" supports, I think I may take them up on that offer when I go to the cancer clinic this week. I always encourage my clients to take advantage of the resources, etc.... . I suppose I better take my own advice.

I shared on Facebook today, and I have received overwhelming support, love, and reassurance. It helps, I think. Thank you to everyone.

More waiting

December 6, 2016

Nothing really new has happened over the past few days. I'm feeling anxious and a bit frustrated right now. I am still waiting to hear what the plan is for tomorrow. I called the Cancer Clinic here at home, and they said they hadn't received the orders yet and directed me to the BCCA. I called them and was only able to leave a message. That planning part of me is a bit frantic, which is unfortunate given the situation is already stressful, but as my dad reminded me, I need to "just breathe." I called and left another message today, so at this point I will wait to hear and do my best to distract myself.

I received some literature on ovarian cancer from Ovarian Cancer Canada that I requested a couple weeks ago. It includes a really great booklet called "By Your Side" that has a ton of great information and has some quotes from other women who have had ovarian cancer. While the information is helpful, I find the quotes reassuring and something that I can relate to. I wish there was a resource like this on the large cell neuroendocrine tumour (LCNET), as this is the cancer I'm more concerned about, but I find the more I try and understand it the more disheartened I feel, so I've decided to leave it be, and trust in my doctors to fill me in on it as needed. My head needs to be focused on getting through the chemo, and while I'm naturally a curious person, I need to challenge that part of myself and just have a little faith that they will tell me what is important for me to know.

I'm feeling a bit tired today, and after doing a couple errands, I think I am going to go rest. Hopefully tomorrow will be arranged soon, and I can have time to prepare myself. Until then, I will try and relax.

WHAT'S ANOTHER WEEK OF WAITING?

DECEMBER 7, 2016

So, as I have been mentally preparing myself for chemo tomorrow, I heard back from the local clinic and BCCA and my chemo has been pushed back a week. I'm okay with it—to be honest, I feel a bit relieved. As much as I'd like to think that I was prepared to start tomorrow, deep down I don't think anyone doing chemo for the first time is 100% prepared. Control in this process is an illusion: this I've come to realize.

The oncologist from BCCA also called me tonight. I have to say that as far as doctors and communication go, I've been extremely impressed. You don't expect to hear from a doctor at 7:00 p.m. in the evening. It was the oncologist that I saw last week who called, and she shared that they had presented my case at their conference today. She said that it was a good discussion, and that there was reassurance that our chemo plan is the way to go. She was surprised to hear that I haven't heard from the fertility clinic, and she said that she would follow up tomorrow morning. We again discussed the potential impact of the chemo on fertility, and it's still a bit up in the air. Everyone is different, and she said that given my age there is still a good chance that after the chemo my right ovary will bounce back. My family and I have discussed it, and I've spent a good deal of time considering my fertility. The decision I have come to is that being healthy in general is more important than my fertility, and that I would rather be alive to have children, whichever way I am able to have them, than to focus on that as a priority and have the cancer come back. The conversation tonight was part check-in and part updating. She reiterated that the PET scan was negative, and that is good news, and what she expected to see. She shared that there was some discussion about the use of radiation in conjunction with the chemo. She indicated that there may be some sort of protocol developed, but that she will follow up with the oncologist that suggested it, hopefully tomorrow. As of now, they all seem to agree that the etoposide and the cisplatin is the way to go: it is the aggressive treatment for an aggressive cancer.

I feel okay about the conversation. I noticed that my chest felt quite tight for some time after. Keith and I debriefed the conversation, as he was a part of it, and I think that I felt anxious only because I think for most of our "date night" I wasn't thinking about it at all. Seeing the number pop up took me by surprise, and instantly my body went into the stress response. We both agreed that it was a good and reassuring conversation, so the only thing I can think of is my body instinctively responded to the stress with tightness in the chest.

Sometimes I still think that this is all one giant mistake and that they will call and say, "Oops, sorry, we had the wrong person." I'm not sure when this thought will go away—maybe once chemo starts, or maybe never. I guess that type of thinking resembles hope, but unfortunately it doesn't really help me. It just makes me feel disappointed and a bit sad. I like to think that I have accepted this, but maybe I haven't, at least not completely. Maybe because physically I feel good, aside from the emotional and mental toll this has taken, which makes it harder to believe that it's real.

Making the Hard Decisions

December 9, 2016

It's been a hard day, to put it mildly. I spoke with my oncologist this morning, as she has been working to get the referral to the fertility clinic under way. I called them, and after a bit of directing, we got it all figured out and I had a 1:25 phone consultation with a fertility doctor in the region. I let my parents and Keith know, and due to the short notice, I fully expected to be on the call by myself, but luckily Keith surprised me by coming home a bit early to be there. As much as I'd like to think I could have managed on my own, I am so grateful that he was there. He truly is amazing.

I had been resigned to putting fertility on the back burner. The conversation with the people closest to me has been that my health is priority, and fertility is secondary. I have been on board with that, but today was definitely a challenge to that frame of mind. There is a chance that the chemo meds will impact my fertility, which we have known from the beginning, but there is still a chance that they won't. Given my age, and my overall health, there is a chance my remaining ovary will bounce back, but no one will know for sure. With that in mind, the fertility doctor gave us two options:

We start the IVF process, and we go to their clinic on the weekend to start the injections. I will have to put off chemo for another couple weeks and go to Vancouver to have my eggs harvested. The difficulty with this is the numbers and the logistics. I only have one, assumed healthy, ovary, which could play a roll in how many viable eggs I may be able to produce, and even then, there are no guarantees. The other is that it pushes back the chemo, which, given the nature of the cancer, is not ideal. The cost is definitely reasonable for the process, but luckily money is not the deciding factor in this decision for us.

The use of a medication called Lupron, which some studies show might be able to "protect" my remaining ovary for the duration of the chemo and may help with preserving fertility. There is no guarantee. This ideally would have been started on Wednesday, but at least if we start now it will have a chance to start working. This will involve a shot once a month.

It's been a bit of a heartbreaking day since then. Keith and I debriefed and talked it through again and again. We left a message for the oncologist to run our concerns by her. Luckily, she's amazing and called us back this evening. She shared that waiting to start chemo is a possibility if I am set on the IVF, but that she would not recommend waiting any longer. She said that given that these types of cancers like to come back, we cannot risk waiting longer than necessary and giving it a chance to rear its ugly head, again.

I struggle with making this decision, because I do not want to regret anything. It's hard to have to make such an important and potentially life-altering decision in amongst all of this happening. I want to live a long and healthy life, and maybe one day I will be a mom, but maybe I won't. I think what I struggle with the most is that the decision would be out of my hands. I have always said that I was not sure if I want to be a mom, and since I met Keith I have felt more sure that I want to be, but I was at peace with the fact that it would be my—or our—decision, and it's now it's not really up to me or us. I don't know what the future holds, but in reality, none of us really do. I may be a mom one day, but whether that's biologically or not is really up to the universe at this point. We've made our decision, and while I struggle with it, and probably would struggle either way, I am ready to move forward. Tomorrow is a new day, and tomorrow is the day we do chemo orientation.

A LESSON IN CHEMO

DECEMBER 10, 2016

Today was chemotherapy orientation at the hospital. We arrived early, which was good, given there were eight patients for them to meet with, including me. It is a strange experience really, knowing everyone carrying an envelope is there to prepare to receive chemo. I was the youngest envelope carrier, and my entourage was the biggest. Again, I am extremely lucky to have the best support team in my parents and Keith.

First, we met individually with the nurse who ran the orientation. She confirmed what chemo meds I would be getting and assessed my arms for good veins. Unfortunately, I have not been blessed with juicy veins, so I will be getting a PICC line put in for my second cycle. For next week, I will have an IV that will stay with me for the three days. It was not initially appealing to me, and still I'm not sure "appeal" is the right word for it, but I like the idea of having the PICC in place for the rest of the five cycles. The PICC line also allows them to draw blood work from it without more needles. I'm already tired of needles, and compared to others I have been lucky, but the less needles the better, especially with my pathetic excuses for veins.

After the nurse, we moved back to the waiting area, and then we were called to speak with the pharmacist. He reviewed my medications and vitamins that I take. A fun fact that we learned today: you are not allowed to drink green tea, as apparently it negatively interacts with the chemo meds. Strange, but luckily, I prefer some Yellow Label tea. Anyways, after that, we went back to the waiting area. Once we were all rounded up, we moved back into the orientation room. The nurse was reassuring and pleasant to listen to; however, I don't think any one can make a PowerPoint of chemotherapy an enjoyable experience. It was a lot of information, and to be honest I'm not sure how much I actually took in. The focus was on side effects—which, if you don't know anything about chemotherapy, are all bad. Lucky for me, Keith takes notes. As much as I try and keep focused and take in everything, my brain tends to shut down, and he picks up the information for me. We make a good team, mainly because of him. In reality, my main role in this has been being the cause of us needing the information, and his role has been to listen to the information and then make sure we follow what we are being told. He really is incredible.

After the orientation we had a fun afternoon, followed by a delicious dinner date with my parents. We are now home to watching some PVR'd TV and relaxing on the couch. It has been a nice and relaxing ending to a day that included an overview of all the miserable things that I can possibly expect over the next few months. It's a strange contrast that I have struggled with these past months, between "normal" life and "cancer" life, since they still feel disconnected to me, but it's the times of normalcy that keep me sane.

A GREAT DAY,
A GRATITUDE DAY

DECEMBER 11, 2016

Today was a good day—actually, it was a great day. We had a nice breakfast and hung out at home before heading off on an adventure ice skating. Keith is a particularly talented skater, while I have avoided showing my lack of skating skill to him. We met up with friends in an impromptu birthday celebration, as my thirty-first birthday is next week. It was a day of laughter, and it felt great. We have been wanting to go for a while, and had been putting it off because of my health, and today felt like the perfect day, and it was. I was reminded again of how blessed I am to have so many amazing people in my life. They acknowledge what is happening, they recognize that it sucks, but then they help to "normalize" it. An example of this, and I'm blessed to say there are many examples, is that one of my oldest, and best friends (who happens to be a nurse) gave me an injection of the ovary suppressant into my butt today. How many people can say that they have a friend who would gladly do that? Well, "gladly" might be a strong word here, but she did it with great skill and an even better sense of humour and made it not something to fear or be ashamed of, but it was as if it was a common thing for us to do, and I felt supported in my decision and at ease.

I was also reminded of the extreme generosity of people. I received beautiful gifts that have helped to lift my spirit and ease some of the stress on my mind. There are not enough words to thank everyone for their support, love, time, caring, generosity, etc... . I am overwhelmed with gratitude, and my heart feels like it could burst. From the quick texts and messages on Facebook, to the huge gestures that leave me speechless, I cannot imagine this journey without the support of the people in my life from near and far. You are all amazing and give me so much strength. While "thank you" does not feel like it does justice to how I feel, it is all I can say for now, so, thank you.

COUNTDOWN TO CHEMO

DECEMBER 14, 2016

Chemo Round 1

Yesterday was my thirty-first birthday. It was a great and productive day. Keith and I reminisced about the last year. It's been an incredible year; even with the stress of the past few months, it has been a year I would not trade for anything. This past year was when Keith came into my life, and in that year, we have had so much fun. I have had amazing times with him and my family, including holding my miracle of a nephew (Quinn) for the first time, travelling to the beautiful province of PEI, being the maid of honour in my sister's wedding in September, and seeing my cousin get married in July. It's hard to not let the last few months define my thirtieth year, but as my dad says, "Even with cancer, life goes on," and he's right. I mentioned struggling with that early on, but I get it now. Cancer, the surgery, diagnosis, and treatment have taken priority over my life for the past few months, but I have to be careful not to let that define who I am or what my life is about. This year has been filled with more love and happiness than I can even think of at any given moment, and it's important to remember that this isn't all that I am or will be; this is a part of my story, not "the" story. I think this will be important to remind myself of, especially in the coming days and months.

I have created a "cancer binder." I probably should give it a catchier name, but it holds all of the information, notes, etc.... that we have collected over the past few weeks. It will hopefully make all of that information accessible in one location, and it has a handle so that Keith can carry it, since my purse already manages to weigh a ton. This is my attempt to be prepared and organized. As I've mentioned, I am a planner, and this is me trying to be in control of something. I suppose learning to let go of my need to control things could be a cosmic lesson hidden somewhere within all of this experience, but until that time, I will do what I always do and "prepare!" I got all of my errands done, again, trying to prepare for not feeling well enough to do those things in the coming weeks. It's a relief, and it gives me a few less things to worry about. Today I cleaned the house, again knocking something off the list of things that was plaguing my mind, and I got a chance to go and visit with good friends. It was a lovely way to spend a cold December day, and to distract me from thinking too much about tomorrow.

Chemotherapy starts in about sixteen hours. It's terrifying, but at the same time I feel like it is a "rip-off-the-Band-Aid" kind of situation. I have been mentally preparing for tomorrow since November 29, and while I know that I cannot actually prepare myself for this, I feel like I've gotten to the point where I am ready to just have it done. My brain has built up the situation so much that I have either grossly underestimated how bad it is going to be, or I have made it so much worse in my head. I won't know until tomorrow, and I'm ready to know. The plotting, and preparing, is exhausting. I've had dreams about chemo for the past two nights, which resulted in a not a lot of good sleep, last night in particular. The first dream—or maybe it would be classified as a nightmare— was about my hair falling out; last night was just about the side effects of chemo. Luckily, I don't recall all the details, but I do recall that much. They've moved my time for chemo tomorrow, which initially I was annoyed with, but thirty minutes does not make much of a difference, and anyone who knows me knows I will probably still be there by 9:00 a.m. since I like to be early for everything. Until then, I plan to relax and spend a quiet night at home, and hopefully get a good night's sleep. Wish me luck tomorrow!

Sitting in chair 4

December 14, 2016

I'm sitting at the cancer clinic getting my second chemo drug (etoposide). I had a long night of tossing and turning. While this resulted in no dreams/nightmares, it has resulted in me feeling pretty tired. I had a lot of nervous energy this morning and was anxious to get here and get going.

It has been a relatively stress-free experience. From the volunteer to the nurses and other patients, everyone has been very kind and patient. The volunteer brought me back to my chair and brought me a warm blanket and a heating pad to get my veins to come to the surface. The nurse reviewed my medications, and I took all of the anti-nauseant meds. I've been pushing fluids, as they say it's important to help flush your kidneys! They put my IV in, which will be with me for the next three days. She used a vein finder, which was really cool, and something that I feel should have been used earlier given my finicky veins. She gave me fluid IV, and then after about an hour, they got the chemo meds started.

It has been a good first experience, which is important. I was very scared, and their reassurance, as well as Keith being with me, has made all the difference.

The volunteer came by again and offered me a quilt. She said they are donated for first-time chemo patients, and I was allowed to pick one. I chose a beautiful one with yellows and maroons and a perfect little square with holly berries, which reminds me of my mom.

The process has gone by quickly since the chemo meds got going. Keith and I chatted in-between my excessively frequent walks to the bathroom! I was a bit worried, since no other patients seemed to have this problem, but the nurse reassured me it's normal. They offered me lunch, which I shared with Keith since I'm not a mushroom soup fan. It's the least I could do for my chemo companion today. I've kept myself busy with my phone, updating people as the time has gone by.

The etoposide just finished (it left a weird taste in my mouth), and they are now flushing the line. I have to pee for what feels like the millionth time. I'm ready to go home and relax. I'm feeling tired, which could be the chemo, or the three nights of poor sleep, and I have a mild headache. At least the proverbial Band-Aid has been pulled off; only seventeen more of these to go over the next few months!

Shared experiences, but different journeys

December 16, 2016

I survived another day of chemo; two down, one to go in this cycle. I feel very fortunate to feel as good as I do, but not to minimize the toll that it takes. I think I feel more fortunate today, if only for the company I kept while in my reclining chair, with my warm blanket and IV chemo drugs. Today I had the pleasure of sitting next to a very charismatic older gentleman and his wife. Immediately upon arrival, you could tell he was a force to be reckoned with. He had a warm and vibrant energy, with a slight undertone of being inappropriate and opinionated. He offered us candy (what he called bribes for the nurses and other patients) and proceeded to chat away. He shared that he hadn't eaten in a week and was hopeful that he might get out of doing his chemo today due to feeling so unwell. He complained of how food tasted different and essentially disgusting, and my dad (my lovely chemo companion for the day, and cancer survivor himself) reassured the gentleman, and his wife, that it was a normal side effect that he too had experienced. This gentleman was delighted (and that's not over-exaggerating) that someone else understood his experience. As we finished up my treatment, they wished us a merry Christmas, and we said that if they were back in January, we may see them again. He informed us that he is "terminal," and that he was not yet sure if he will have a sixth cycle of chemo. I imagine it's not an uncommon conversation on a cancer ward, but it still struck home how even though there is a shared experience, we are truly on our own unique journeys.

I am grateful for how well I do feel in comparison to other people's experiences. I do feel exhausted, I have a headache that starts in the morning after taking my three medications to prevent nausea and vomiting, and I have experienced hot and cold flashes, but I consider myself lucky that I can manage those symptoms with relative ease. It may get worse, who knows, but it may not. Time will tell, as part of what makes this journey unique for everyone is that chemo effects everyone differently. I received another medication to take as needed in the evenings, which will also help manage nausea and also possibly help with the headache. I struggled with the headache last night; as I mentioned, you cannot take Tylenol, aspirin, or ibuprofen without permission from a doctor (due to their ability to cover up a fever, and also their impact on the stomach, liver, and kidneys), but by the morning I felt a bit better. I was slightly nauseated, but I made myself eat some breakfast and drink a lot of water to better prepare my body. Hopefully these new medications will help as intended.

For now, I am going to get more rest. I got to "talk" to my nephew (he's not quite one and did not have a lot of words for me—just smiles, which I gladly absorbed), and that has lifted my spirits more, but now I'm tired again. Tired I can handle; I've always been one who likes their sleep, so I will go and take care of myself. Until tomorrow.

Day 3/21 complete

December 17, 2016

The last day of chemo for this first twenty-one-day cycle is complete. Today felt more tedious for some reason, from drinking enough fluids before I left the house, to managing my IV, to sitting in the chair for a few hours. I didn't sleep well last night, which probably didn't help, but in the end I made it through. I had a bit of an issue with my IV today, in particular the area around it started to get cold, and they warn that cold, hot, tension, burning, etc.... are not good signs, and that they may have to do another line, luckily with the aid of a heating pad I made it through without having to get another IV put in and though the cisplatin infusion (usually thirty minutes) took a little longer, it went off without issue. My dad was again my "chemo companion" today and watched over me while I slept. And I slept this round, falling asleep for the majority of my etoposide infusion (forty-five minutes) and through the fluid flush at the end. I woke up just in time for the IV to be taken out and for me to head home.

While I still feel like the symptoms are manageable, I was definitely thankful for the new medication for breakthrough nausea in the middle of the night and this morning. My appetite is still good, though for no reason I'll think of a food and find it immediately unappealing, but I have to eat to take my medications, so luckily, I can still manage to eat what I find appetizing.

I have eighteen days before my next cycle starts, and I am hoping to rest up and be ready for it. I have been told to expect a bit of a crash over the next few days as the medication with a steroid in it will be tapered off, and my body will have to resume making its own, but luckily it's the weekend and Keith and I can relax and there is no stress to do anything but rest.

I have another appointment scheduled at BCCA in Vancouver in the new year with a radiation oncologist. I am trying to move it as it falls in the few days after my next three days of chemo, and I don't think travelling to Vancouver will be the best thing at that moment, so hopefully it can be pushed back a week or two. We have heard rumblings of radiation, so I am hoping that this consultation with let us know what the plan is. It's another part of the evolving plan, and it will be nice to have an idea, as fertility issues will again arise with the discussion of radiation.

Anyways, I have made it this far, and am feeling more encouraged and prepared moving forward. I know that it's not over, but with the support I have I know that I can make it through these next few months no matter what this journey throws at me.

Cycle one: day four— not my favourite so far

December 18, 2017

Day four kicked my butt a bit—well, maybe more than a bit. I definitely felt unwell yesterday but managed to make it through without vomiting. Physically it felt reminiscent of when "Felicia" was present, specifically the nausea, which started first thing. The medications help, but there was an undertone of feeling sick and tired all day. The nausea unfortunately reared its ugly head whenever I went to eat, which resulted in changes to what I could stand to eat at any given moment. Thankfully, Keith has the patience of a saint, because I changed my mind from one moment to the next. The smell of food cooking just doesn't have the same allure that it once did, but I find if I don't make my mind up until the last minute I'm pretty good.

I'm not sure if some of it is in my head, since they give you an idea of what to expect, but generally my goal is to listen to my body and not push it too hard towards anything that makes me feel unwell. I am trying to balance my need to rest and listen to my body with not being a pest. I try and putter and do things around the house, but I feel a lack of energy and motivation that I'm not used to, with the exception of the time the tumour was present. My brain feels fuzzy sometimes, my stomach sick, my skin extremely dry, and my body tired. This is only cycle one, so I'm getting a better idea of what to expect, though I have to say day four has been the hardest so far. Hopefully today will be better, and I am looking forward to the possibility of bouncing back a bit with the arrival of family this week for the Christmas holidays!

FINDING ZEBRA PRINTS IN UNEXPECTED PLACES!

DECEMBER 20, 2016

They warned that days four to six could be a "crash," and they were pretty accurate. As I mentioned, day four was filled with a lot of nausea, and day five was off-and-on nausea, but day six took it out of me. I went to town with my mom, to do a little last-minute shopping and I was taken off guard by how quickly I got tired.

I started off the morning okay, even though I didn't sleep well, being up throughout the night peeing. I try and keep my fluids up, but unfortunately, I paid for it all night long. I got up and felt a bit nauseated so didn't eat right away but had a few crackers and some orange juice (a safe bet these days) before leaving the house. I ate later in the morning, and it was delicious, but my stomach still felt off. We carried on with our errands, and by around 11:00 a.m. I was exhausted. I am somewhat used to having low energy since this all started, but I was surprised how quickly my energy left and how my legs felt like jelly. I felt silly with my mom trying to find us a close parking spot, giving her my lecture about how "I need the steps …" and "it's good for me …" but I can honestly say I was glad we weren't parked at the end of the lot when we were done! By the end of our journey, I stayed in the car until we made our way home. I am grateful to have such understanding people in my life, and to remind me that I don't have to be a "superhero." I find it's easy to get down on myself for not doing the things I used to do, whether it's because of a lack of energy, or nausea. I want to be able to cook, clean, work, exercise, etc... . the way I could only a few months ago. It's hard to not be able to do those things without thinking of timing, energy, and whether my stomach will tolerate the process of cooking or the smell of cleaning products (both of which have been an issue over the past couple days). Again, I'm very fortunate to have such amazing people in my life to reassure me that this is normal and will pass. Their patience with me has been appreciated.

This afternoon, I took advantage of being able to relax. I didn't nap like I expected, but while I can be very tired sleep doesn't always come easily. I caught up with one of my best friends and my nephew via Facetime and enjoyed seeing their faces. Laughter and smiles always help lift the mood. Tonight has been much the same as the others in this cycle so far, basically just taking it easy. As the holidays approach I am just taking it one day at a time and enjoying each day.

I did have kind of a cool moment this morning. One of the errands I went on with my parents was to their doctor's appointment. While we were sitting in the waiting area, there was a TV broadcasting ads and health information (i.e., make sure you exercise thirty minutes a day, etc... .) and on came an ad for NETs (neuroendocrine tumours)! Until November 29, 2016, I had never even heard of NETs, and here there was a full ad discussing them! If you haven't heard about NETs before, that is one of the types of carcinoma that "Felicia" was, and while it's a rare condition, it's becoming more known. You can look up more information on http://www.cnetscanada.org if you are interested. It was just strange to see it up there for all the people to see! It was something that until a few weeks ago would have meant nothing to me, and now when I see zebra prints, it catches my attention and I instantly pay attention. The zebra print is the NET ribbon colour (like pink for breast cancer or teal for ovarian cancer). It's kind of a neat story, actually. My sister found it out for me shortly after I was diagnosed. They say that doctors are taught that "when you hear hoofbeats think horses, not zebras," because typically symptoms point to common illness (horses) not rare ones (zebras), but unfortunately for many people, this can result in missing the diagnoses for those zebras. Anyways, I just thought it was a neat moment, and it made me feel connected in some strange way— as if someone else might be sitting in that waiting room today and know what the zebras were all about. I know there are lots of people out there with NETs, not necessarily in the ovary, but I haven't met any since my diagnosis, and it made me feel like there is this community of people out there. I am going to try and find out more about CNETS Canada and see if I can find others with the ovarian version. That was one of my goals in starting this blog, aside from keeping people updated and processing this journey for myself. There may be a herd of my zebra people out there, looking for my particular stripes too!

IS THIS REALLY HAPPENING?

DECEMBER 21, 2017

Yesterday I had an okay day, overall. I had a burst of energy in the morning, made breakfast, cleaned, and did some other chores around the house in-between, taking various breaks. By the afternoon, I was paying for it and slept for a couple hours. I have a few new side effects, or what I assume are side effects of the chemo. My skin hurts—or at least, that's the best way to describe it; it could just be body aches. I've noticed other weird changes to my body, particularly that my skin on my face is weirdly soft, my hair feels thicker yet oilier, and my skin colour looks off to me. I think there is an element of being angry with my body for all of this, and that makes me scrutinize it and judge it. I know my body did not ask for this, but I suppose there is a part of me that holds it responsible in some unreasonable way.

I've struggled with feeling disconnected from myself particularly since chemotherapy started. I sometimes feel like this isn't happening to me, like it's still not real. I feel terrible, but that's because of my empathy for "this person" who it is happening to. I know that it's happening to me, but at the same time it still doesn't feel true. It can't be. I can talk about it matter-of-factly; I know the process, I go through the motions of the appointments and the treatment, but yet it still feels surreal. Maybe that's why the side effects have been harder to manage over the past couple days than I had expected; they are the physical reminders that this is real. I can't escape it. I'm already in it, cycle one has started, and it can't be reversed. My body is being attacked by the chemo drugs, and so is hopefully any remnants of the cancer (if those microscopic little cells are in fact there trying to hide).

I find that my hormones are off, and I get emotional easily. I'm trying to keep that in check, but I also think I have pretty good awareness that I can cry for no reason. That being said, after a good cry and conversation with Keith last night, I recognize that I have reasons to cry and that's okay. I try not to get sad or let the "why me" creep in, but they got in last night—and, really, cancer isn't fair. It's not fair to anyone. Not to the person diagnosed, or the people they love, or who love them. This is the struggle, I guess, the flow from sadness, to fear, to anger, to acceptance, to grieving life as it was a few short months ago. I can't make things go back to the way they were, no matter how much I want that, because ultimately this is where the road leads, and at least on this journey I have the best of travelling companions and as much of a guide map as I can hope for.

Happy Holidays!

December 27, 2016

I haven't blogged for a few days, but it has been quite busy with all of the Christmas events. I am so grateful that I felt as good as I did. I struggled with side effects of the chemo, but I pushed through and enjoyed time with family and friends and celebrating Keith's and my first Christmas together. We were spoiled by each other and our families, and it was nice for my brain to focus on something other than cancer and chemo.

Family Christmas Breakfast - Stephanie, Jerrad, Rick, Hayles and Keith

The side effects of the chemo have luckily been relatively mild, but they have included fatigue, hair thinning, nausea, some hot flashes and night sweats, poor sleep, anxiety, and a headache. I haven't had much nausea, except some this afternoon. The headache has really been the worst part, since I can't take anything for it. I make sure to stay hydrated, as I know that can play a role, and a warm steamy shower and sleep seem to help, but otherwise it has been pretty constant over the past few days. Today the fatigue has hit me pretty hard. I had the best night's sleep that I've had this past week last night, but by 10:00 a.m. I was sleeping on the couch and slept off and on all afternoon. I think the last few days caught up with me, and my body made the decision to rest whether I wanted it or not. I missed out on a family get together today, but truthfully, I don't think I could have managed it. Even the idea of having to walk upstairs to the bathroom was exhausting, let alone getting dressed and going out. Luckily, a lot of my family lives nearby, so I can catch up with them fairly easily. Also, I think my hair is starting to thin. When I had long hair, I would "shed" like crazy, and since cutting my hair off I haven't had that problem. Lately, the odd hair comes out when brushing, etc... . but generally nothing of concern. However, over the past two days, I have noticed when washing my hair that I will get quite a few strands coming out. I feel a bit panicked by this, but I've been mentally preparing myself the best I can. The panic may have some relation to the anxiety I have been experiencing. I have had anxiety at times throughout my life, but I have noticed an increase in that lately. It scares me sometimes, because it causes tightness in my chest, which makes me more anxious, as heart issues can come with the chemotherapy. I am always able to manage it, using all the skills I've taught my clients over the years, but it's still a struggle some days.

I heard back from the Cancer Agency the other day about radiation. I am a bit confused now, but they were quite friendly. I was told that radiation may be considered, but that they weren't sure yet. I received an appointment with the radiation oncologist for a consult in early January, but I was trying to move it, as it falls in the few days after chemo, and based on how terrible I felt this past cycle, I was not prepared to travel to Vancouver in that time frame. So, I called to move it, and they wanted to set up both the consult and the first appointment to prep for radiation. I tried to explain to the woman that I wasn't even 100% sure I am supposed to have radiation, so I wasn't sure if we needed to set up that appointment yet. After a bit of conversation, even she seemed a bit confused, noting that I am only in my first of four to six cycles of chemo, and radiation wouldn't happen for at least four weeks after my last cycle, if it happens at all. She said that she would follow up with my referring doctor and get back to me. I'm leaving it in her capable hands and will let you know what the plan is for radiation in the future. I'm trying not to worry about this, as there is nothing I can do about it right now, and I'm reminding myself to take it one day at a time and not get caught up in the "maybes" and "mights."

Anyways, I am again quite tired, so I am going to rest before the World Junior game starts (Canada vs. Russia). I hope you are all well and are enjoying the holiday season!

Again, with the hair!

Well, what I thought was my hair falling out a few short days ago was more of a false alarm, or possibly a precursor to today's events. My scalp started to really ache last night, like that strange feeling when your hair is parted in one direction and you run your hands through it against the grain. It doesn't hurt so much as feel strange. This is the only way I can describe this feeling, but it has progressed from "strange" to full-on discomfort. Then, after my shower, in which the warm water felt nice on my scalp, I tried to brush it and gave up on that due to how it felt. I started to blow dry my hair, since my dryer brush is out due to the bristles hurting my scalp, and that's when it started: hair, more hair than your typical shedding, falling out. Single strands, groups of strands congregating in the sink. I knew this could happen, and would most likely happen, that was part of the motivation for cutting my hair (aside from wanting to donate it chemical-free), but there is nothing that quite prepares you for that much hair coming out in one sitting. There are a lot of emotions around my hair, as I've mentioned previously. I've struggled with my short hair, and despite the reassurances from people in my life, I don't like it. I want my hair back. It may seem silly, and unimportant, and in the grand scheme of life I know that it is, but I took pride in my hair; it made me feel pretty and feminine. And now, it's just a reminder of what is happening, a reminder that my body is under attack. Unfortunately, it's going to get worse before it gets better, and I know, I know, it will grow back. Until then, I will manage the sensitive scalp and do my best to keep my shedding hair to myself.

I got a timely and wonderful gift today from one of my best friends. It's the book *Brave Enough* by Cheryl Strayed (she wrote *Wild*). I have always loved quotes. There is something about quotes that makes me feel connected, it's a reminder that someone in the universe felt the way I am feeling, or thought what I am thinking at some point in time. The quotes in this book spoke to me on many levels, and the little notes she added in made me smile and, admittedly, tear up. One in particular was, "If it is impossible for you to go on as you were before, so you must go on as you never have." I feel this struggle a lot, maybe even a bit more with the hair issue. I don't think I can go through this journey as I was before, because nothing I've gone through has truly prepared me for this, not even my dad surviving cancer. This gives credence to taking it one day at a time, and I think that is the way I "must go on." I need to leave the planner, and the control freak, and the impatient part of me behind, as they were as I was before, and go forward living in the moment and enjoying life as much as possible, as it is happening now, even if it means finding a silver living in losing my hair.

Happy New Year!

January 2, 2017

Today is the beginning of a new year. The New Year is a time of reflection, looking back on the past year, and a time of hope looking forward.

I've reflected a lot these past couple months, mostly with fond memories of the past year, including spending time with my family and friends, falling in love, working with people I respect and genuinely enjoy working with, travelling across Canada, getting to see my nephew grow from 1 lb 9 oz to an adorable little one year old, being a part of two weddings in my family (my sister in September and my cousin in July), hiking, ziplining, kayaking, spending time at the lake, etc... . Even with all of these amazing and wonderful things, I find it hard to not let myself get into that ever-popular mindset that 2016 was a terrible year. But truly, it wasn't a terrible year, even with a diagnosis of cancer and the commencement of chemotherapy, it really was not as bad as it could have been. It was a year of more peaks than valleys, and I try to maintain that mindset instead. Life changed drastically, don't get me wrong, and if I could choose I would obviously choose to not have this happen to me, but it did, and now we deal with it.

This leads into hope for the future. 2017 is not going to be an easy year, that much I am sure of. It's going to be a challenge, and as my sister says, "an experience," and I hope that this time next year chemotherapy, at least, is a distant memory. Not that I am wishing away time; in reality, I am grateful for time. Time is healing, or at least that's how I'm trying to see it. I am hopeful that this next year brings more time with the people in my life, and more of a focus on enjoying them. I hope to be able to do most of the physical activities that I enjoy, even if I have to give up a few (such as slo-pitch—at least for the spring season). I plan to spend time at the lake and in nature and enjoying time with my dog (who is getting used to having me at home). I hope to get back to work and do what I enjoy and work with people who make going to work that much more enjoyable. Cancer gives you perspective, it has made me slow down and I plan to take advantage of that.

I brought in 2017 with Keith and Liam (our eleven-year-old black lab). After four days of my hair falling out in handfuls, more so even this morning, I made the decision to shave my head. We laid down newspaper in the kitchen and invited my parents over. I admittedly cried just sitting in the chair, even before the clippers buzzed to life. I cried because I don't want to be bald, I cried because it sucks, and I cried because I want my long hair back. All things that really cannot change, and will not change by shaving, or not shaving, my head. My mom talked me down from the proverbial ledge, and after a few hiccups with the clippers (which my superstitious side said as a sign not to do it), we got under way. It's a moment I will most likely never forget. At one point, my mom was cutting my hair with scissors to make it easier to shave, and Keith and my dad worked with two sets of clippers at the same time. Eventually, my dad took over, which was slightly karmic, given the number we did on him when we shaved his head due to chemo hair loss twenty years ago. We laughed. It is important to be able to laugh, and cry, when you need to, especially in moments like this. I am happy to say it doesn't look too bad. I have a few light patches where you can see a bit more hair has fallen out in comparison to other areas, but not to brag, but I think I have a fairly good-shaped head. It's pretty round. I remember thinking after touching it for the first time, *That's my head*. Keith had gotten his hair buzzed off yesterday, so I had been rubbing his bristly scalp, but it still felt weird. It was my head. It was another disconnected moment, and again I'm not 100% sure I've connected to it yet. I expect a few more moments of tears and panic in the coming days, but it was the right decision, and I will learn to rock the GI Jane look the best I can. And luckily, I have such great supports that both Keith and my dad both shaved their heads with me so I am not alone in the shaved-head look.

Deciding to Shave

I am forever grateful for all of the people who have supported me thus far, both in person and on social media. I am sharing this journey, and it's nice to be reminded daily that I am not alone.

Anyways, I wish you all an amazing 2017, filled with happiness, health, and love! Take care of yourselves, and until next time, Happy New Year!

PICC DAY

Today was another big and long day. I had my PICC put in this morning. I was really nervous, again not knowing what to expect. My mom was allowed to be in the room with me, so it was helpful to have a familiar voice (as I was lying down and couldn't see much). The nurse was great. She explained everything and was very reassuring. That being said, it was not my favourite experience I've had throughout this journey. It was uncomfortable even with numbing, and honestly, my arm is in so much pain right now I'm starting to wonder if the IVs might have been the better route! I like to think short-term pain for long-term gain. I felt quite anxious through the procedure, which is reasonable, I think, given the fact they are feeding a tube towards your heart. It took about forty-five minutes from walking in to leaving, the procedure itself taking about twenty-five to thirty minutes. It's very high-tech, which is nice given the explanation of how it used to be done. Anyways, it's in, and the pain should go down with the heating pad after a few days. It'll involve weekly flushings at the home health office, which is kind of annoying, but they will be able to draw my blood pre-chemo, which will make it easier than having to go to the hospital.

I met with a new doctor today, a GP in oncology. She was great; very reassuring. She checked in around side effects of chemo, did an exam, and reviewed my blood work (which came back good, although I'm a little anaemic, which isn't uncommon for me despite taking iron supplements and vitamin C). I was able to express some of my frustration with the talk of radiation. I received another phone call this morning about booking a consultation and first appointment for radiation. This is again frustrating to me, as I am only to have a consult to discuss the need for radiation, yet I'm being asked to book it, in Vancouver (three hours away) and for the day before my third chemo cycle is supposed to start. It's not all that frustrating in the grand scheme of things, but honestly, after having the PICC put in and the discomfort I was (and am) in, it was more than I could handle at the moment. The new doctor said that she would follow up with my oncologist in Vancouver and find out what's happening with that. I am not against radiation, it's just that the timing is terrible, and given that we had discussed the possibility of harvesting eggs after chemo and before radiation, it's confusing and again frustrating to me that I don't know what's going on.

I tried on wigs today too. That was actually pretty fun. I don't mind the shaved head, not nearly as much as I thought I would. It makes for a very quick shower, and it takes no time to get ready in the morning. I like the idea of a wig mostly for fun, and maybe for occasions where there are little children that I know who might not understand what is going on. Plus, it allows me to experiment with hair colours and styles I would never have been confident enough to try before.

Hayles Cool Purple Wig

Anyways, that's where today landed, and I am feeling pretty good about the start of cycle two, which commences tomorrow. Wish me luck!

CYCLE TWO: DAY TWO

JANUARY 6, 2017

Already two-thirds of the way through the chemo portion of cycle two. It's much less stressful this time around, now that I know what to expect. I have been lucky to have two great chemo companions this cycle: my mom and my uncle. They have kept me company, and the 2+ hours have gone by very quickly both days. Again, I am blessed to have such amazing support take the time to be with me, and all the people who offer. I wish I could bring them all, though I'm sure the nurses would have something to say if I brought an entourage to their busy ward!

Today was the first day where I saw another young person there. It might sound odd, but it was kind of reassuring in a weird way. I didn't interact with her, but I was more aware of her presence than any other patient on the busy ward today.

The side effects of the chemo have been okay, manageable. I had the headache again, which they said is a side effect of the one medication, but again I can deal with it. I stay hydrated and get rest and take time to be in the quiet if that's what I need. I woke up around midnight last night and felt nauseated, so I took my other medication and that helped. I definitely don't sleep well during these three days, waking up and not able to fall immediately back to sleep, but I try and make it up with a nap, which I haven't had in the past couple days (I hope that doesn't sounds as silly as it does to me: "Poor me, I didn't get a nap for two days!"). The thing that

I find chemo does to your body is that it will catch up eventually, whether you want it or not!

I am happy to report that my PICC is settling in well. It's bruised and still hurts slightly, but it's definitely healing and not even close to the pain it was two days ago. I have to say, it does speed up the procedure when you have it; they can hook you up right away, and there is no messing around. I suppose with the volume of patients in and out each day, it's a godsend for the nurses. Anyways, I am going to rest and watch the World Junior gold medal game between Canada and the USA, not that these types of games are remotely relaxing for me, but I feel the need to support Team Canada! Until later …

THE DIFFERENCE A YEAR CAN MAKE ...

JANUARY 8, 2017

Today is cycle two: day four. It has been a good day, a day with nausea and fatigue, but a good day nonetheless. In the past year, there have been many dates that have stuck in my head: October 3, 2016, the day the tumour was found; October 27, 2016, the day of my surgery; November 29, 2016, the day I was diagnosed with ovarian cancer and a large cell neuroendocrine tumour; and December 14, 2016, the day of my first round of chemo. All days with some negative connotation, but the day in the past year that I am choosing to focus on today is my one-year anniversary with my boyfriend.

This day, one year ago, I went on my first date with Keith. It was the beginning of a great year, and the beginning of an incredible journey, which I am grateful for every day. As I have mentioned, many times, I am blessed with all of the support in my life, from my parents, my sister and her husband, the rest of my family, to my amazing friends and coworkers. Keith is another amazing example of this.

On October 3, 2016, when we found out that the symptoms I had been experiencing and the mass in my stomach was something to be concerned about, and when the first time the possibility of cancer was even mentioned, I gave Keith "an out." As we walked out of the hospital, I told him I would understand if this was too much for him, and while it would hurt, I would understand if he wanted out. He listened to my offer and promptly shut it down. Over the following months, I would continue to tell him how amazing he was/is for sticking through all of it, being there for me, and he would easily respond, "It's what you do when you love someone."

We have been through a lot in the past year, mostly in the past four months, more than most couples go through in years and years together. We've talked about this past year, with a focus on the past few months, and what it has meant for our relationship. I think after seeing my parents go through this similar type of experience twenty years ago, I take their advice. My mom said to me, "Include him as much as he wants to be … it feels helpless, and if he wants to help, let him." And while my instinct was to protect him from what I am going through, he has shown me that I am stronger with him. He has been there every step of the way, he has shown up, he has taken notes at appointments, he has asked questions I couldn't or didn't think to, he has held me when I cried, he has encouraged me to feel what I need to feel, and he has not hesitated to support me. I am thankful every day that we went on that date 365 days ago, and I am thankful every day for Keith being in my life, and I am most thankful that he is the man he is.

CYCLE TWO: DAY SIX

JANUARY 10, 2017

Today was a "lazy day." Not in the sense that I didn't want to do any thing, but more that I physically felt incapable of doing anything. Today was definitely the most I've felt physically beat by the chemo.

I found during the last cycle that on days one to five or six I didn't sleep well, and these past five days have been no exception. I know that I sleep, but the second I open my eyes, I feel like I haven't actually been sleeping.

I woke up tired this morning. I got out of bed, made breakfast, and saw Keith off to work. I have tried to maintain some semblance of routine through all of this, so even though I'm tired, I get up and do my usual routine, getting dressed, etc.... . Today, as soon as Keith left, I made my way to the couch with my book and fell asleep for an hour or so. This was followed by periods of being awake, reading, watching TV, listening to music, more napping, talking to my sister, and dealing with a few calls and emails about coverage, benefits, and medications. That was about all I could handle today. I hate that part of this. I hate not having the energy to go shovel snow, or to go for a walk to the mailbox, or to even putter around the house. I know this part passes, or at least it did last cycle, but it's hard to not get frustrated feeling like a lump!

I get my PICC cleaned tomorrow, and I can honestly say I'm looking forward to that! Woohoo! The highlights of chemo treatment, a PICC cleaning and bandage change! I know I've only had the thing for a week, but honestly, it'll be the best day when this thing comes out and I can have a proper bath or shower, without Press 'n Seal wrap around my arm! Plus, it'll probably be nice to get out of the house tomorrow and get some fresh air. Until then!

Down, then up

Today was a much better than yesterday, and it's nice to be able to say that. Day seven for these two cycles has been the hardest by far. It is the day when I physically hurt, I can't stop eating yet feel nauseated, and I am exhausted.

Yesterday I slept extra, and at one point was cognizant of sitting on the couch staring into "the abyss." Okay, that is slightly overdramatic, but honestly, I caught myself staring into space in silence multiple times. I can't tell you a lot about what else I did, but I know I sat still for most of the day. I had no interest in TV, movies, reading, or listening to music. I barely made it through phone calls, abruptly ending one to say, "I need to go nap again." I recall getting up and going to the bathroom, looking in the mirror and thinking to myself, *I look and feel like a chemo patient today.* My skin was pale, my balding head was pale, my eyes felt grey, and my body ached. This was made more difficult by knowing I had to prepare myself to get much PICC cleaned. I am incredibly lucky that my amazing uncle was willing and able to come get me for my appointment. In my wisdom (I use this term very sarcastically), I had planned to "not be a bother" and take the bus into town for the appointment. This plan was quickly proving to be a terrible one, given my physical state on day seven and the fact that it was -25 here yesterday. Uncle to the rescue, and I made it to my appointment warm and safe and sound. It felt very good to have the PICC cleaned, and it helped to boost my spirits to be outside even for a short time.

Today I woke up feeling about 90% better! I had energy and felt more focused and interested in things than I have in awhile. I baked! I haven't baked since probably before "Felicia" was found, and it felt really good. I had rest times, and I napped, but I felt genuinely good. I made dinner for my parents and Keith—something I haven't had the energy to do for a while, though I had a bit of a system for this; I slowly prepped everything throughout the day, including making rice this morning, cutting onions a while later, grating cheese a little later, etc.... until everything was prepped but just needed to be put together. It worked very well, so this is a bit of a life-coping mechanism I can use hopefully in the future. Plus, it makes cooking so much faster when everything is prepped like that, like a cooking show! I got to spend some one-on-one time with my dad as he volunteered to help me cook if I wasn't up to it. It's nice to talk to him about chemo/cancer stuff because he gets it, but he also doesn't let me sit in it too long. Plus he's probably the only one who can make me laugh when he tells me my hair is falling out in a "cul-de-sac" like a balding old man! It's reassuring to hear him relate to the fear and worry of each ache and pain being cancer, or a bad sign, etc.... which can be a tiring and unconscious thought process. It's nice to have his experience to rely on and help me through mine.

I do have a bit of a cold it would seem, which started yesterday, but so far, it's manageable and I'm keeping an eye on it. I hope that I continue to feel this good but will be mindful that energy comes and goes, and I still need to listen to my body.

Cycle two: day eleven

January 15, 2017

It's been a pretty low-key few days. I ended up going to the doctor earlier this week after some concern about the cold I seemed to have. I had difficulty breathing while lying down, which led to not getting much sleep Wednesday night. I was able to get into the doctor that morning and get checked out. I ended up having a chest X-ray and doing some blood work. Everything turned out well, and the cold has taken it easy on me since. The awareness and concern about my health is something that has changed for me throughout this experience. I am more acutely aware of what's happening in my body; however, I am also far more paranoid, as well.

Other than that little blip in my health, I have been feeling better each day. Still get tired in the late afternoon early evening, but I've continued to take it easy this week—partly because doing too much still makes my chest hurt, but also because I want to conserve my energy for various plans I've had this weekend.

My hair continues to fall out in eyelash-length hairs. I find that my scalp is easily dried and gets quite itchy. I did some research on what works for a dry scalp, and most websites and forums suggest staying away from normal shampoos, and most suggest almond or coconut oil. I currently am sitting on my couch with coconut oil rubbed into my scalp, and I have to say it feels quite nice. This is just another one of those things I never thought I'd

79

have to consider or worry about! I've been lucky to have my mom help with my hair/scalp these past few days. As I struggle to scrub my own scalp in the shower due to the plastic wrap around my PICC, she has been washing my scalp in the sink, and massaging oil into it. It has also helps to get some of the hair off my scalp. I'm not entirely bald, but close enough. I got my new cotton caps and my lavender wig this week. I have tried to wear the wigs over the past couple days, but my scalp is not in love with them at this time. They are fun and make me feel a bit better about not having hair, but they take some getting used to. The cotton caps are nice though, so I'll continue to wear those when out and about or when my poor head gets cold.

CYCLE TWO IS FLYING BY!

JANUARY 20, 2017

Things have been pretty stable these past few days. I ventured out on my own again on Tuesday to have my PICC cleaned. It was a quick process, and very much needed. I'm still having discharge (sorry for the yucky visual) from my PICC site, which they say will tone down as the weeks go on, but it still kind of grosses me out. Luckily, I don't have to see it very often with the sleeve covering it. It was nice to have it cleaned and to get some fresh air. I spend so much time at home, and for good reason, but it can feel a bit confining some days. I stopped by work and visited with co-workers. It's nice to see them and be around there. It makes me want to be back at work more; to feel like I'm doing something and contributing to the world and my household, etc... . in some way. Many co-workers have been great supports from sending me hats, cards with positive messages, and well-wishes, to bringing Keith and I food, and making me coconut oil mixtures for my scalp. I'm, again, very lucky for all of the support and kindness I have in my life and am grateful for it all.

This cycle is coming to a close, and it feels like it has flown by. It's weird to say that, but compared to cycle one, this one feels like it has gone by quickly. I know there is still another six days, but I'm not ready for the next one—or at least I don't feel all that ready. I don't "dread" it, but I'm really not looking forward to it. The last week has been pretty good symptoms-wise, so maybe that's the part I am struggling with looking at next week. I have been able to go out on my own, I've felt tired every day but that's been manageable, and I was even able to go out for a walk last night, which felt amazing. Prior to "Felicia," Keith and I used to walk almost every night from twenty-five minutes to an hour, and since October I have gone for a walk once, until last night. The cold snap we've had hasn't helped with that, but after having a long nap yesterday and a rise in temperatures, I was able to go for a twenty-five-minute walk. I felt good, exercise felt so good, and given that most days I don't have that kind of energy, it left me feeling "normal" and maybe a bit exhilarated. I am hopeful that come Tuesday I will get the news that I only have to do four cycles, and that will mean I am halfway done and just that much closer to getting back to my normal life routine!

An emotional
kind of day...

January 24, 2017

Today was my appointment with the doctor at the cancer clinic. It went pretty well, but emotionally and mentally I am feeling pretty raw. It looks like we are sticking with the six cycles provided my body continues to handle the chemo as it has these past two cycles. That part I'm not shocked about, I had hope that it would be lowered to four, but the skeptical part of my brain was prepared to hear six. Obviously, I would have preferred four, but then again, I obviously would have preferred not to have to do any of this at all. Other than the six-cycle news, things are much the same physically. My side effects from the chemo are "normal," lymph nodes seemed to feel normal, and lungs sounded "good," all good news.

Radiation was discussed again. I've, for some reason, been extremely overwhelmed by the idea of radiation, even more so than the idea of chemotherapy. I've struggled to understand why, and I figured out that it was maybe just that it fell in line after the diagnosis, and the treatment plan of chemo, but I think today I realized that I have avoided the idea of radiation because of what it means for the future—in particular, what it means for my future fertility. I've talked about this before, and the struggle I had in making the decision to start chemo vs. doing IVF. The trouble with my diagnosis of large cell neuroendocrine ovarian cancer is that there is no procedure to follow for treatment, there seems to

83

be a lot of unknowns, and even the doctors are basing their planning and ideas on "cancers that behave in a similar way," but really no one knows what's going to work or not work, and that is frustrating. Today we talked about where radiation fits into the overall treatment plan, whether it's better to do radiation alongside chemo or wait until chemo is done, etc... . Based on the information I got today, radiation is looking like a foregone conclusion. It has been shown in "cancers that behave in a similar way" that radiation is the best chance to prevent any movement to lymph nodes (which is apparently where this type of cancer really likes to travel to) if there are any microscopic cancer cells still lurking around and surviving the chemotherapy, and I want my best chance of not having to do this ever again. The best chance of a cure is what we're looking for, but the risk to my fertility is the other potential outcome that I am struggling with. No one can tell me what the statistics are on the possible effects of chemo on my fertility; they can only make a guess. The guessing leaves room for hope, and I've found that while hope is important, it also hurts when it dwindles. I have clung to the idea that even if the ovary that is left survives the chemo that I could possibly harvest eggs from it and eventually carry either my own biological child or, with the use of a donor egg, carry a child that would be mine but not biologically. And while I haven't heard it straight from the radiation oncologist's mouth, I was told that most likely the radiation would fry my ovary and make my uterus inhospitable to both a harvested egg and/or a donor egg.

It's hard to hear these things, and it dims that light of hope of ever being a mom more and more, and that's when this whole process gets more difficult to process and be okay with. It's when I hurt the most, I think. It's one of those things that makes me so angry and so sad, and I don't know what to do with that. There is no one to be mad at, no one to blame, it just is what it is. I know there are exceptions to this, that people have been able to have children after chemo and/or radiation, but nothing says that I get to be an exception. Maybe I used up my "exception card" when I got this stupid rare cancer in the first place, and when it comes to fertility I'll be the rule. No one can tell me, and as probably anyone who has had cancer—or any health issue, for that matter—can tell you, the not knowing is one of the worst things. Radiation feels like the end of the line, like there is no turning back, and really chemo shouldn't feel much different, but somehow it does. I know there are other avenues to being a parent, if that's what we choose to do, but I feel like I'll miss out on things, and when it's not your choice to miss out on those things, it's heartbreaking. I'm blessed to have my family and Keith, and I know that they will support me no matter what, but I'm not at a place where I'm okay with it yet, and I don't think there is anything anyone can say that will make it okay. For now, I get to be sad, and I get to cry, and it gets to hurt.

CYCLE THREE: DAY TWO

JANUARY 26, 2017

Day one of this cycle was rough. It started out well. I drank about a litre of water, my chemo companions were my aunt/neighbour and my uncle, and the time in the chair seemed to fly by. I found out that I have been referred to a radiation oncologist in Kelowna instead of Vancouver as it's easier for me, so I am now waiting to hear from them for an appointment, hopefully in the next couple weeks. According to my doctor, the sooner we can do radiation, the better chances of cure are. I can't argue with that, as that has been the goal from the beginning. However, this might mean taking a break from the chemo after this cycle (if they can arrange things in time) to do radiation, and sandwich it between the first three cycles and the last three. I'm more resigned to the radiation now, though it still hurts my heart to think about the big picture of what it means. It will take time to process, and that may include talking to someone outside of my support system to be able to accept it in my own way.

Back to yesterday. By the time I got settled at home, it felt like a typical day seven, with a day one headache, which if you've been following along is a terrible combination! I'm not sure why it hit me so hard. I lay down for a while and eventually managed to have some lunch and a bath (which helps with the aches/restless feeling in my body), and then I slept for a little bit. I woke up a bit startled, thinking that I had missed an appointment or had something to do that I was forgetting, but I realized I had nowhere to be but the couch. This was a pleasant realization. I stayed on the couch pretty much all day, even when Keith got home. I had no appetite, so he made himself some dinner and we watched a bit of TV. Admittedly, I fell asleep again for about forty-five minutes. By the time I had to take my evening medications, I had to eat something whether I wanted to or not, so I settled on a glass of milk and a wrap folded in half with peanut butter and honey. It hit the spot. I ended up going to bed at my usual time and was worried sleep wouldn't come due to the steroid and my napping, but eventually it did. I woke up at various times in the night but fell back to sleep without issue.

This morning the alarm failed to go off, but we managed to get Keith out the door on time, and I feel good again. My energy, which could very well be the steroid, feels good and my appetite is good (I had a bowl of Cheerios), and I'm mentally preparing myself for the day. I have a weird metallic taste in my mouth, which happened the last couple cycles, but it makes even drinking water a chore. Luckily, Keith got me a wooden spoon for Christmas that allowed me to avoid a stainless-steel spoon for eating my breakfast so that made eating a lot easier. Chemo is at 10:00 a.m. this morning, and again my amazing family has stepped in to help out. My aunt is driving me in and keeping me company, and I think my uncle may come again as well. I am ready for these next couple of days of chemo to be done, then the chemo can do its job, and then I might get a little reprieve between now and whatever the next phase of the plan turns out to be!

Cycle 3 Kicking
My Butt (a bit)

January 29, 2017

Today is day four of cycle three. This has been the toughest cycle so far, though it's only a few days in. Day one, as I mentioned, I slept most of the day. Day two I had a lot of nausea, but I didn't nap after chemo or sleep well that night, and yesterday, I slept the day and the night away (aside from my frequent trips to the bathroom). Today was another day of fatigue and nausea. I woke up, had breakfast (which, luckily, my nausea didn't impact), did a few things around the house, and by 10:00 a.m., I was napping on the couch until around noon. I can't even feel frustrated with myself for the amount of sleep I've gotten over the past four days because my body has not given me a chance to dispute it. One minute I'm watching TV, and the next I'm waking up from a long nap. I decided to go to town with Keith this afternoon, and though it was tiring, I'm glad I did. It's nice to get out and get some sunshine and fresh air. I also had to pick up more anti-nausea meds, which are imperative at this point of the cycle, at least that's been my experience over the past couple months and cycles.

Today, Keith and I also watched a web-ex program called the "Big Cancer Hook-up 2017" put on by an organization called Young Adults Cancer Canada. It was a neat opportunity that I heard about via Facebook, and I am really glad we signed on. There was an event here at home, but unfortunately due to the side effects of the chemo this time, I did not have it in me to attend, though hopefully there will be others like it in the future. Anyways, the program had three speakers talking about their experiences being young (aged fifteen to thirty-nine) and having cancer. Though none of them had the same type of cancer as I do, I felt like I could relate to them and their experiences. There were a couple clips teasing about CTs and PET scans, etc... . and it's weird to be able to relate to those things in that way, but it definitely made me laugh. It's nice to know there is a community out there for people in my age range, and people that can relate to the experience of being young and having cancer.

One of the things that stuck out to me was the last speaker. She talked about expectations with herself, and that possibly other people have of younger cancer patients, after treatment. She talked about the expectation that when she was done chemotherapy and radiation that she would head straight back to work, and life would get back to normal. You'd get back to working, eating, exercising, socializing, etc... . the same as you did before. This is something that I have struggled with, because I am motivated to get back to work as soon as possible and get life "back on track." There is a part of me, pre-radiation discussion, that thought, *My last cycle should end in April, and I can be back to work at the beginning of May.* I admit, there is still this thinking present, and I struggle to not see life getting "back to normal" as soon as humanly possible, but given that no one really knows what will come from all of this treatment, and what my cancer journey will be, I think I have to start letting go of "back to normal" and accept that this is "my normal," at least for now. What comes in the future will come, and I need to be in this moment and let that be enough for now. I can't plan ahead, no matter how much I love planning things, as the universe seems be trying to teach me a lesson in being mindful and patient in a big way. I might as well start to listen, and maybe letting go of some of those expectations I have of myself, and I perceive others have of me, whether it's returning to work right away, being able to work out, the fertility stuff, etc.... . might make this part of the journey a little easier. It's all part of the journey, I suppose, but opportunities like today make it interesting and make the journey feel a little less lonely. #YACCHookup17 (www.youngadultcancer.ca)

GETTING THROUGH THE "ROUGH DAYS"

JANUARY 31, 2017

As I've mentioned previously, days six to eight tend to be the hardest days of the cycle. I'm feeling tired, achy, a bit nauseated, and I have been having the "eats," as I call them. Once the steroids stop, my appetite kicks up a hundred degrees and I can't seem to not eat everything in sight! I've made an effort to have veggies and other snacks easily on hand, which helps, but it's hard to keep my appetite under control. I've been mostly resting today, after doing a few household chores this morning. It's weird to feel restless, yet tired. It's like my body cannot make up its mind.

I've got my appointment with the radiation oncologist for a consult for next week, and a scan to have my radiation "marker" done right after that. We will have a little travel to the appointment, but at least not to Vancouver this time. I'm expecting to feel better by then, at least if the last couple cycles are any indication, which is better timing for travel. I've become more resigned to the radiation piece, but I am still not looking forward to yet another procedure and treatment.

To radiate,
or not to radiate...
That is the question

February 9, 2017

Side note: I'm not one to complain about the tests, and I will happily do what the doctors suggest or ask, and this may be an over share, but when you've had two gynaecological exams in about two and a half months, it gets to be a bit cumbersome. Today I opted out of that exam, which the doctor was very understanding of. I realize that having a gynaecological cancer means I'm bound to have more of these exams than the average woman, but honestly, I was not mentally prepared for it. (I'm actually a bit proud of myself for speaking up.)

Anyways, back to the important stuff. So, here I am, with my some of my amazing supports, in an exam room, prepared to be told that the fellow didn't know what she was talking about and that radiation was still the plan, and accepting that my uterus and my surviving ovary are going to be roasted, and that is not how it played out. (Another side note: my questioning the fellow is based entirely on the way I had envisioned today going, and definitely does not speak to her competence. She seemed very intelligent, and was extremely lovely, and knowledgeable). The doctor came in and basically said that he was not sure why we are using radiation. He said that based on my pathology, the research that they had done, etc.... . that there was no evidence to support radiation in conjunction with the chemotherapy, and that surgery and chemotherapy has been shown to be the best treatment for cancers like mine. Again, there is no protocol, because large cell neuroendocrine carcinoma of the ovary is rare. So, this is where I get a bit confused, as I've now been told two different things. One being the news today, which is obviously what I had been not so secretly hoping to hear, but at the same time had convinced myself that radiation was the plan, and that my fertility was toast, and that was that; the other thing being that radiation and chemotherapy are the best combination of treatments (aside from the surgery I have already had). The doctor said that he will take my case back to the gynaecological cancer team and discuss my case again and see if they "can convince" him that radiation would be beneficial. So, now we wait some more. I'm cautiously happy, but also still preparing myself for the team to be able to convince him (though his arguments were sound and made a lot of sense to all of us). It's a classical case of "hope for the best but expect the worst"— something I have gotten very good at these past few months. We will have to wait until next Wednesday (the team meets Tuesday nights), and it will be tough to not let that hope creep in and take over, but I don't want to be crushed if he comes back and says, "Oops, I was mistaken, radiation is needed."

If they were to say that I need the radiation, I think I would opt to have my uterus and right ovary removed (if that's an option) instead. They would have no function after the radiation anyways. The risks of radiation are more than I was even aware of, and though they are "rare side effects," they sounded a bit more than I am prepared to handle at thirty-one, including changes to bladder, bowel, and rectum function (which may or may not resolve itself), the potential for the pelvis and bones in that region to "fracture" for no reason, the potential to develop a secondary cancer later in life, etc.... . Those were the highlights. It's hard to find the benefit in that given they tell me that they got all of the cancer. Anyone who knows me knows I pee more than the average human, and that I am clumsy enough on my own; I'm not prepared to have to pee more than I already do, or possibly fracture a bone by just sitting still!

I struggle with what I am supposed to feel right now. I know that there is no right or wrong way to feel. I want to embrace the hopefulness, to sit in it and let it absorb into every fibre of my being, but I can't. If the doctor says I have to have radiation, it will be one of the hardest things to hear, especially after I had prepared myself to hear it today. I think any experience like cancer nega-tively impacts that optimistic, take-things-at-face-value part of a person. I feel most days like I'm waiting for the other shoe to drop. I went from living my life, having a great job, working full-time, living with my amazing boyfriend, going out with friends, making plans, spending time with family, taking care of myself, to having had cancer. It was out of me before I even knew what it was, but it changed everything. One day, one doctor's appointment, one ovary changed everything, and while I knew that things happen, life happens, cancer happens, I never expected it to happen to me. I think I'm still trying to reconcile that. Not so much the "why me?" but just that it happened and is happening. No matter what happens next week, I know that I will be okay, and that we will get through it. It just felt good to have some good news, even if it is possibly short-lived. Until then, I am going to enjoy feeling good this late in cycle three, and mentally and physically prepare myself for cycle four of chemotherapy to start next week.

IT WAS A GOOD NEWS KIND OF DAY!

FEBRUARY 16, 2017

It has been a long few days, filled with me sleeping a lot. I had been making an effort to get exercise in on the days I was feeling up to it, as I've managed to do the opposite of what you'd expect while on chemotherapy and have gained weight. It's hard to maintain a healthy lifestyle when you experience fatigue 21/21 days of a cycle. Not to mention exercising in the morning means I'm done for the rest of the day, and one of the meds make appetite go all wonky, and for 2/21 days I eat nonstop. Not the "I-have-no-willpower" kind of nonstop, but the "I-become-physically-uncomfortable-and-feel-sick-if-I-can't-eat-in-that-moment" kind, sort of like what I imagine a zombie would be like (thank you steroids for your anti-nausea abilities, but more sarcastically, thank you for your unfortunate appetite stimulating properties!). The unfortunate thing is those four days of exercise and being out and about each day resulted in sleeping most of Saturday, Sunday, and Monday. This wasn't entirely bad; actually, it was very wonderful, as I got to see some of my wonderful friends, got some fresh air, and was able to get a bit of exercise, but I also got to enjoy some relaxing time with Keith and my ever-loving old dog, Liam. Listening to my body, it clearly told me that it needed the time to recuperate, most likely in preparation for this week, the commencement of the fourth cycle of chemo.

I feel like a whiner, and though Keith reassures me that this is not the case, I was dreading starting another cycle. I would have thought it would get easier, yet somehow this is not the case. My first cycle felt like it went smooth and was better than I had envisioned (i.e., I was not vomiting all day and night like I expected—thank you to the marvel of modern medicine and the four anti-nausea meds that do the trick). However, as each cycle approaches, I dread the feeling tired, nauseous, achy, and ravenous for food, the weird taste in my mouth, and the foggy brain, etc.... . I liken it to knowing you are going to have the worst flu, but there is nothing you can take to prepare yourself or feel better. The only consolation this round is that when the sinus congestion starts I was told I can take an antihistamine! Yay for small victories! (That is not meant sarcastically, either, I'm genuinely happy about that). But on to the good news.

In my search for silver linings, I realized that my dread for the upcoming cycle allowed my brain to put waiting for the radiation oncologist's phone call on the back burner of my unfortunately simple brain. Side note: chemo brain is a real thing; honestly, I can count on both hands the amount of times today alone I was listening to someone, heard nothing of what they said, and had to ask them to repeat it. Anyways, I digress (damn chemo brain again). I had been so stressed about seeing the radiation oncologist last week, but somehow, I hadn't thought much of it over the past couple days, until we were on our way to chemo this morning. We were expecting the call at 3:30 p.m. as scheduled, and to the benefit of our inpatient selves the doctor called at 12:45 p.m. instead. I don't really know what I had expected him to say, and actually initially misheard him, much to the high level of stress poor Keith had to endure only hearing my side of the conversation, and my one-worded responses. I thought the doctor had said, "I wasn't able to convince them," and I think that I immediately shut down; however, then he said that the conference (the lovely group of people, I'm assuming they are since they help treat and save cancer patients, who reviewed my case again) voted "95% in favour of *not* recommending radiation." So clearly "wasn't able" was actually "must have been able to convince them"! He reiterated his previous sentiments, "There is no tumour to radiate," "I'm not sure what I'd be directing the radiation at," etc.... . Though he did graciously offer that "If you really want radiation, I can do it," to which I said, "No thank you!" So, in the months of doctors not giving me good news, today was a break in that pattern, and I got to hear what I had been hoping and praying, and what many others had been hoping and praying for me, to hear. I do not have to have radiation. Radiation would be an option in the future if the cancer was to return, but for now we will stick with the plan and complete the last three cycles of chemo. There aren't words for how relieved I am, and how much more hopeful I feel about the future. There are no guarantees in life, this I know, but feeling a piece of that hopefulness get slowly extinguished was one of the hardest parts of this journey. But that hope is back, and it feels amazing! I want to say a huge thank you to everyone who has been sending me love and saying prayers for me. I truly believe in the power of healing and positive energy, and I am grateful for all of you!

With that good news, I felt a renewed sense of energy, which unfortunately didn't last long. I wasn't even sure that I would have the energy to blog today, but I also wanted to let people know the good news. Plus, the few hours I slept this afternoon helped to give me a bit more energy than I had when I got home. The side effects about the meds (the headache in particular—thank you, Ondansetron) have started, but they are doing the trick to manage any nausea, so I'll take the trade-off. I feel tired, my brain is, as I mentioned, foggy, and I've felt a bit physically wobbly. I will get through these last three cycles, there is no doubt about that. My body is taking a beating, but after today my spirits are higher and I feel more ready to fight on. Plus, I have a huge team of support behind me, and I know their encouragement drives me forward. I'm blessed in so many ways, but no way more than the support I have in my corner. Love to you all!

Cycle 4: day 6

We are into cycle four now, and today was a rough day. As those of you who follow my story know day six/seven tend to be a challenge. Today started off with a headache, upset stomach, and nausea, which to anyone, anywhere, is an unpleasant way to start the morning. I pushed through and tried to be somewhat productive in my "routine," and made Keith breakfast, but that was the extent of my morning. I took my medication to help nausea, and pretty much stuck to the couch all day. With the exception of getting my PICC cleaned and bandage changed, I didn't move far. Thankfully, my amazing uncle was able to drive me, since this is a day I definitely needed the help. The cleaning went well. I've been a bit stressed about my PICC lately. It was being a bit fussy during chemo, and by fussy I mean it wasn't allowing blood to flow back (which is not good), and at one point the flush wasn't going through, but we managed to get it figured out. Today I found out that it has pushed out of my body about 1.5 cm, which doesn't seem like a lot, and apparently is not a huge deal (they say they usually give it 2–2.5 cm wiggle room before X-raying it). I stress about the PICC because I hate it, and I don't want to have another one put in, ever. It just needs to make it until March 31, which by my calculations will be my last chemo day (provided no surprises)!

"The eats" started last night, so with the nausea this morning I had a bit of a reprieve, but they returned full force later in the morning. I honestly feel like I cannot adequately explain the discomfort of the appetite stimulant portion of the whole steroid experience. I feel so unwell, but so incredibly and constantly hungry, and it's as though my brain convinces my body that if it eats it will feel better, but that never happens. It is a vicious cycle that I cannot wait to be over. I wish I could sleep through these days and wake up not feeling like that. I try and keep track of what I eat in an effort to be more mindful, but honestly it makes me feel worse to see what I can eat on one of these days. I really hope that it tapers off tonight, which seems to be the case given I haven't eaten since dinner about 2.5 hours ago (this is a big stretch on an "eats" day).

I find my mind moving towards the future more now and focusing on the things to look forward to. When this all started I found it was important to not get too far ahead of myself and keep to the day to day outlook (sometimes minute to minute), and maybe it's better to maintain that, I don't really know. Maybe because it feels like there is a light at the end of the tunnel I am able to allow my brain to go ahead. I'm not inundating myself with things to do and plans to make, but even through the next couple cycles, and through the end of this one, I find myself more looking forward to seeing people and going out, and being outdoors, and going on little adventures. I've struggled to be social and positive, and am so grateful for the encouragement and connection of my friends who have reached out to me, even when they didn't know what to say, when I have had nothing to share, and even when I cancelled plans because I didn't feel up to going out/couldn't go out, etc.... . I've appreciated all the patience and kindness that has been sent my way. I'm really looking forward to times with friends, a visit from my sister and my nephew for the next couple weeks, upcoming birthdays, art nights, a trip with Keith to meet his sister, etc.... . Just spending time with people who make my life more meaningful and doing things that make it more worthwhile.

I know there is still time between now and the end of cycle six, but it's hard not to get a bit excited. I know that there is still two more cycles of feeling like I did today, and possibly worse, but I'm ready to feel better, and move on from this part of my journey.

Feeling Better, and a Bit Introspective

February 23, 2017

I am feeling a lot better today, and it's nice to feel it, and recognize it. It's easy to notice when I'm not feeling well, since those are the side effects that people ask about and that Doctors get concerned about, but I'm trying to make sure that I recognize the ways in which I'm feeling good. Today I was able to tidy around the house and not take a nap (not to brag, but I've gone three days without a nap)! I ate more than my body needed, but the eats have subsided a good deal (thankfully). I was able to go out with friends and feel comfortable and just enjoy their company. It's such a gamble most days, but it feels nice when I get a day like to today.

I had a great chat with my dad today too. It's nice to get his perspective on things and be able to talk about things that other people might not quite get, not because they don't try or want to, but because it's a bit of an experiential understanding. We talked about the end of treatment, some of my anxiety about the future, and we talked about how it feels harder as the time goes on. I think I've mentioned this before (chemo brain might play a role, since I cannot remember if I have written about it or just talked about it), but I thought going through each cycle would get easier, but it feels like it has been harder. Not necessarily the physical part, though that plays a role, but more the mental part. I remember dreading the start of cycle four a little over a week ago, but I'm already starting to get that feeling for the next cycle and there is still a ways to go. I know that there are "only" two more cycles left, but my brain is already starting to go to that negative place. We talked about how no one really talks about the ending treatment part of chemo/treatment. He put it into perspective for me, saying that it makes sense that it feels harder because when you start treatment there is a goal. There is a task to be completed, and in my case, this was six cycles of chemotherapy. As you move towards completion there feels like there is a void after the fact, the unknown. I imagine it a bit like an abyss where it feels like my purpose changes again, but it's the unknown that makes me feel uneasy. Prior to this cancer journey starting, my motivation in life was my family, my boyfriend, my dog, my friends, my home, my work, etc... . and finding out I had cancer and needed treatment changed that in some ways. Not that those things were, or are, no longer important, because they are the very things that keep me going, but with my diagnosis and treatment plan things shifted. I had/have a task to accomplish, a motivation, a goal to strive towards, but what happens when it's over, or when it's supposed to be over? I feel like I'm supposed to go back to life as I knew it, but there is this feeling that I can't ever go back to life as I knew it, because it doesn't exist anymore, at least not without cancer in the picture in some way. For the past 142 days, cancer and treatment have been my reality, and though I'm well aware that the world has not stopped for me and that life continues to happen, I guess I will need to take the time to process what it all means for me moving forward, and how I need to make sense of this part of my story.

THE EVE OF CYCLE FIVE

MARCH 8, 2017

It's been a really nice week. I have had a chance to visit with my sister and my incredible little nephew, spend time with family, meet more of Keith's family, and spend some relaxing time with Keith. I've been lucky to feel good and be able to really enjoy those moments.

Tomorrow is the start of cycle five. I have that dread feeling, and what I think is some anticipatory nausea and a headache that won't quit. I saw my doctor through the cancer clinic for a check-up, the appointment I have before each cycle. We talked again about the end of treatment, and it makes me feel hopeful yet anxious. She confirmed that I get my PICC out on my last chemo day, March 31, so that was some great news, and I booked my last three PICC cleaning appointments (yay!). I will hopefully have a chance to talk to both my doctor here and my oncologist in Vancouver before cycle six starts so that we can organize the follow-up plan. As I mentioned, we discussed follow up every three months, but she said that given my diagnosis they may change that a bit, so we will wait to know the exact plan. Until then it's just getting through the next few days and crossing another cycle off the list, but the countdown is on! (Twenty-four days till last day of chemo and PICC removal; forty-two days till the end of cycle six!)

Cycle five is under way!

March 12, 2017

Cycle five officially started on Wednesday. It has been a fairly typical cycle so far, though I admittedly feel more nauseated than I have previously. My medication seems to help somewhat, but overall it hasn't completely removed the feeling in my stomach. My appetite is low, but I have been able to eat, which is good. My three days of chemo went well, though my PICC was giving us a bit of trouble. I had great company across those days with my mom, one of my amazing aunts, my amazing uncle who has consistently shown up for chemo, and of course Keith. The company makes the 2–2.5 hours go by quick, which I appreciate. I am grateful that my chemo only takes that long, and is not a full-day process.

We are definitely on a countdown now. Only three days of PICC cleanings left and three days of chemo before the end and before my PICC can come out, so I'm just crossing my fingers that it makes it to the end of the month for that to happen. At this point if it doesn't make it, I'll take the IV to finish treatment off, my poor veins be damned!

I've been feeling somewhat more anxious again, having a slight meltdown earlier this week, and I think I've figured it out a bit more clearly in my own mind. I am looking forward to the end of chemo—I cannot wait, in fact, for it to be done—but at the same time, it's a slightly bittersweet thing. There is an odd sense of safety with knowing chemo is coming. What I mean is it is almost protective in nature. Generally, and hopefully, if you are on chemo, your cancer cells are either shrinking or not growing. Once chemo stops, your body gets not only a chance to heal and recover, but there is that fear, in my case, that it could start producing cancer cells again. The fear of recurrence. I have looked at various forums, research, etc... . and so far, it does very little to calm my nerves and ease my mind. I try and use the skills I have to refocus my thinking to stay in the present moment, but it's hard sometimes to keep those thoughts at bay. I want to focus on getting better, feeling healthier, going back to work, living life, but sometimes the fear gets the best of me. I don't think these fears will go away for a long time, but I feel a bit more in control being able to recognize them and name them. It's just tough some days, but as with every other part of this journey, I will take what comes and do my best to work through it. Until then, we are in the home stretch with cycle five underway, and cycle six setup for the end of the month.

Plugging Along

Cycle five is admittedly kicking my butt. I knew that there was a likelihood to have the side effects of the chemo get worse, but I think I took for granted the relative ease at which I felt I got through the first three cycles, and really the fourth. I am well aware that it could be much worse—I am very fortunate to be doing as well as I am—but this cycle has been hard.

The first three days were again difficult. I felt nauseated, had a headache, felt exhausted, and overall just terrible. I slept a lot over the weekend, getting as much rest as my body could take. I still get completely thrown by how tired a person can be by simply "doing nothing," though I recognize that while I am not physically moving my body is doing plenty in this battle. The last couple days have been a struggle, as usually the nausea passes a bit sooner, but the body aches, the tiredness, etc... . have started to ease a bit today. I am still going through "the eats" as of today, but I feel a bit less horrible having given myself a more routine eating pattern. I am also trying to go for a walk around the yards a few times throughout the day. Now that the snow is almost all gone and the weather is tolerable, I am enjoying the fresh air. My body is entirely deconditioned, it just feels like an all-round mess, and my history of back pain is starting to rear its ugly head, but I am slowly going to build back up my strength and little walks help me feel more capable.

I have to get a chest X-ray done this week, as my PICC line has "migrated" 2.5 cm now. They will do an X-ray to see if it's still able to do what it needs to do in order to finish off cycle six. I'm a bit annoyed with the whole thing, but at the end of the day I can appreciate that stressing about it will not change anything. Either it'll work, or it won't. I only need it to last one more blood work and three days of chemo! They've also moved up my hearing test to before cycle six, which is reassuring. I still have the odd episode of ringing, but overall, I think it's okay.

Anyways, I am still plugging along, and am hopeful to keep feeling better each day. Feeling more positive has been easier to come by with the promise of spring floating around. Bring on the sunshine!

PICC-LESS AND LOVING IT!

MARCH 23, 2017

Today was a step in the direction of being done; unfortunately, it came a bit too soon, but it is both good and bad. I got the news yesterday that my PICC had migrated too far and is therefore unusable for chemo next week. While this is inconvenient from the point of view of finishing my final cycle, I am elated. As you know, my love–hate relationship with my PICC has been primarily a hate-based affair. I was able to coordinate the PICC being taken out in the community, instead of at the cancer clinic, and as of 4:00 p.m. today that sucker is gone. I was shaking with anticipation yesterday when I got the news, and didn't sleep well last night, but it was worth it. For anyone who might ever need a PICC, I can honestly say the removal was nothing; I literally felt nothing. In fact, the only thing that was uncomfortable was having the PICC bandage removed from my skin! I have a pressure bandage on it for twenty-four to forty-eight hours (let's be honest, probably closer to twenty-four) and then I can shower and bath without "Press 'n Seal" or a cast glove for the first time since January 3. The only bad part of having it removed this early is that I will have to get a needle for blood work instead of having it taken from the PICC and I will have to have an IV put in for the three days, which is how my first cycle was delivered. Hopefully my veins withstand the three days, and it'll only be the one IV needed. Fingers crossed.

It is almost a bit deceiving, the feeling I have, having had it removed early. I have to keep reminding myself that there is still three days of chemo left next week (which will be done with an IV). If I feel anything next Friday like I do having just had the PICC removed, I will be the happiest of people! It's hard to believe all that stands between today and finishing chemo is one blood test, a hearing test, an IV and three days of chemo!

THE COUNTDOWN IS ON ...

MARCH 27, 2017

Today is the last weekend before cycle six starts. It started out as a very rough cycle, but it turned out to be fairly good by the end. Those first eight days were the hardest, but the last week and a half was almost worth it, almost. I have been able to go for longer walks, enjoy times with family and friends, and enjoy springtime. I have particularly enjoyed the PICC-free life. The skin on my hair is still recovering, but it's been truly wonderful to have it gone.

This weekend has been fairly good. I've found that in the last few cycles the weekend before chemo starts I get tired and nauseated. I call it "anticipatory nausea and fatigue," as though my body is preparing for the upcoming onslaught of chemicals. I have napped quite a bit over the past couple days, so hopefully it has given my body a chance to prepare. While I've been resting, my hair continues to grow back and, as it did when it fell out, it aches. People often ask if it itches. I'm not sure which would be preferable, but I haven't had any itching, just the aching feeling where new hair is coming in. It's grown back quite a bit, but still has a long way to go. I liken my current hairstyle to that of a baby elephant, thus including the picture of a baby elephant for reference.

Hayles Wig Testing

Anyways, I've been getting that anxious feeling again, which I also relate to chemo starting. I have to remind myself that if all goes like it did last cycle, it'll be a week or so and I'll hopefully be on the mend until the official end of the cycle. I know that it seems like a short time, but if you've ever had chemo you know that those days of feeling horrible are not something you can easily overlook and pretend they aren't coming. This cycle setup is a bit unkind really, because you feel so horrid for that first week, sometimes longer, and then start to feel better just in time to get hit again. You never get enough time in-between to really forget how terrible you are about to feel. However, having met various cancer patients, I am keenly aware that it could be worse, so I try and maintain my gratitude for only six cycles and just overall access to treatment and medications to try and make me not feel quite so bad.

I'm still unsure of what "after chemo" will look like, and when I get to go back to work, etc.... . but my goal is to start with exercise, eating right, and giving my body a chance to repair itself before I get too far ahead of myself. My body, physically, has taken a huge hit, and it's going to take time to regain strength, stamina, etc.... . I'm looking forward to working on that, and to just feeling healthy and strong again.

Tomorrow I am going to do my blood work, as I do before chemo each cycle. Then Tuesday is the hearing test and my appointment with my doctor at the cancer clinic. Fingers crossed that it all turns out well and I can get cycle six over with.

ON HOLD

MARCH 29, 2017

We are currently at a bit of a standstill. I had my hearing test this morning, and that went well. My hearing is within normal limits, which is great news. For those who don't know, one of my chemo medications, cisplatin, can attack nerves, including those in your ear. As a result, hearing changes and/or loss can be a side effect. As I've mentioned in the past, I have had episodes of ringing in my ears and one occasion of "hearing drop" where I woke up and couldn't hear anything. While this can happen for patients receiving this medication, it's most likely that once chemo is finished this side effect should improve. It's just good to know that it's still within a good range.

This afternoon, I met with my doctor for my usual check-up before chemo starts. Unfortunately, this is where the standstill comes in to play. My blood work was not good, at least not good enough for chemo to start without a hitch. The protocol I am on requires certain levels in my blood work to ensure that my body can handle the chemo, and again unfortunately the numbers are not high enough. So, as of right now, we are waiting to hear from my doctor here at home, who is planning to speak with my oncologist at the BC Cancer Agency about a plan. If I don't hear from her tonight, I am supposed to get blood work in the morning and see if my numbers have improved. If they have, then I will start cycle six as planned. I may end up getting an injection that might help with the numbers, and/or I may end up having to wait a week to start my last cycle. This is disheartening. I am trying to stay positive, but it's quite frustrating—particularly given that this is supposed to be the last cycle. The finish line is in sight; I just hope they don't move it.

Cycle six has begun

My numbers were up yesterday morning, thankfully, and cycle six of chemo started. I really wasn't sure what was going to happen, but thankfully the finish line went nowhere! It was a really long day yesterday. I got to the hospital just before 8:00 a.m. to get my blood work done, and luckily there was no line-up. I got that done quickly and headed up to the cancer clinic to wait for the doctor. The clinic wasn't even open when I arrived, but once the doors opened I hung out there until my doctor arrived and gave me the thumbs up! My neutrophils were 2.0, and even my haemoglobin was up from 99 to 105. I hung around until my appointment at 10:00 a.m.

My amazing uncle showed up to keep me company and to drive me home. Company makes the time go by much quicker. It took longer than usual because I needed the IV put in, and given my veins have a habit of running away and hiding it took a bit of effort and a vein finder (my new favourite technology), but we got it! We finished chemo around 12:30 p.m., and my uncle brought me home. I felt okay, but a bit tired. I had lunch and slept for the rest of the afternoon. My energy was immediately zapped once I was lying on the couch. Once Keith got home, it took every ounce of my energy to just go upstairs to the bathroom. I didn't even have it in me to blog. Dinner was cereal, mostly because I had to have something in my stomach to take my medication, and even that was exhausting to eat! It was early to bed knowing that I usually don't sleep well on chemo nights. I slept on and off all night and was up early this morning. I feel much better than I did last night, which is usual for me. Mornings are typically a good time for me, which allows me to have my main meal of the day since my appetite goes downhill as the day goes on.

Chemo is at 1:00 p.m. today. Not my favourite time, but not much I can do about that. One of my amazing aunts is taking me today, so I'll have great company again. Then tomorrow is the final chemo day! I can't wait to feel better and celebrate!

CROSSING THE
CHEMO FINISH LINE

APRIL 2, 2017

Yesterday was the last day of chemo for cycle six (the cycles are twenty-one days, so this cycle will technically end April 18). It was a great day; I don't think it could be classified as anything but a great day. I woke up and had a delicious breakfast made by Keith and we headed into town. We stopped and got some treats for the cancer clinic staff as a little "thank you" for all the amazing work they do, and how wonderful and compassionate they have been; and we delivered them before my chemo appointment. I was lucky to have one of my amazing best friends be my chemo companion for the day, which again helped the time go by as quickly as it can. We had a bit of trouble with the IV again, only two pokes though! That took my total to ten this week, and I can admit I was extremely happy to have that part over with. I never thought I'd get to place where getting an IV or a needle would seem normal, and though they pinch or can be painful, they don't bother me nearly as much as they once did.

We ran a few errands after chemo, which my energy level tolerated. I think the excitement of no more chemo boosted me up a bit. I got a chance to rest, and then had a mini impromptu celebration with family. It was nice to recognize the day as being something to celebrate, and if I've learned anything over these past almost seven months, it's that it's important to celebrate and be thankful for those moments. I'm looking forward to a celebrating more when I am ready.

Last night the chemo hit me a bit harder, thus no blog. I recall sitting on the couch around 8:00 p.m. after having another IV and saran-wrap-free bath (grateful for the little things!), and that's about all I recall between episodes of waking to tell Keith I was going to bed, only to fall back asleep within seconds. I say this often, but being that tired still surprises me! Finally, after a couple hours of sleeping and waking, and stating my intention to go to bed, Keith ushered me upstairs, where I promptly fell asleep. I was up throughout the night, as is common on chemo days and the days following. I woke around 3:00 a.m., wide awake (thank you, steroids) and nauseated (thank you, chemo) and took some medication before eventually falling back asleep. I am grateful for the medications in times like that.

Today has been okay. I have been tired, and quite nauseated. I've eaten a bit and got out of the house for a little while. I try to get out when I have the motivation, as I know over the next few days I won't be going anywhere, as usually my side effects increase. I am tired, though, and I sense this cycle will take it out of me, as the fatigue in particular seems to accumulate each time.

I still can't believe that chemo is done. I don't think it will feel completely real until the end of the cycle, but I am grateful to be done and grateful to have made it through as well as I have. Don't get me wrong, there is nothing easy about chemo, nothing, but I have been extremely fortunate in my experience compared to others.

As for what happens next, I really can't say for sure. I am supposed to hear from the oncologist's office about an appointment for three to four weeks from now, and hopefully then the follow-up plan will be figured out. Most likely it will include another follow up every three months for the first year. I'm okay with that. I'm just ready for life to move forward, for my hair to keep growing back, and to get back to a normal and health-focused routine.

I try not to get too far ahead of myself. Recurrence is always on the back of my mind, as I understand is the norm for most cancer patients. I work to not let my head go there too often or stay in that space too long. In reality, until the three-month check-up happens, there isn't much to be done, so wasting energy, time, and thoughts on that wouldn't change anything. If anything, it only serves to take away the happiness and good things in my life that I want to be enjoying each day. For now, I will focus on rest and recovery, and try and get some fresh air and sunshine when I can.

CYCLE SIX HAS COME TO AN END

APRIL 19, 2017

Today is the official end of cycle six. It arrived without any fan fair. As quietly as this cancer journey began, the treatment portion has ended. As I check in with myself, I feel emotionally tired. I would have thought "happy" would have been the primary emotion, but rather I feel a bit drained. Don't get me wrong, I am extremely happy that chemo is finished—in fact, I couldn't be happier to be done, but when I stop and think about it, "happy," surprisingly, wasn't the first feeling that came to my mind. It's possible that there was the anticipation of chemo starting again, which I think becomes ingrained in your mind and body and leaves you feeling tired before you even get started. Maybe tomorrow it'll hit me when I don't have to take any pre-meds or prepare myself to go to the hospital.

I have been feeling a bit better each day. I still have some side effects of the chemo, including numbness in my toes and some tingling in the very tips of my fingers, pain in my hand and arm where the IV was for the chemo, fatigue, and the mental fog, etc... . but it's easier each day. I've had some discomfort in my abdomen where my ovary/Felicia were removed, which sends me into a panic at times, but I remind myself that I have had this in previous cycles, and it was okay. It's hard not to go into panic mode with things like that now. It's one thing that I really struggle with since my diagnosis, because I don't want to live in fear or be a hypo-chondriac, but I also don't want to minimize anything since my uncanny ability to minimize is what took me until looking almost eight months pregnant before seeing my doctor. On a better note, my hair is growing back in earnest now—just a few thin spots left. I think I look more GI Jane-esque than a baby elephant now

I have been pushing myself over the past week—not every day, but when I feel like my body can handle it. I still had the crashing over the weekends, which has been normal throughout chemo, but it felt good to get those days in where I did not need to nap or was able to exercise. I had my first 10,000-step day since October 3, which felt amazing. I even went on a hike, which was a huge challenge physically, but with Keith's support, encouragement, and ultimately his incredible patience, I was able to hike 0.8 km to a beautiful waterfall. It was a struggle to recognize just how bad my physical ability, strength, stamina, and endurance has fallen. When we arrived, I literally scoffed at the 0.8 km (twenty minutes each way) sign, since that would have been nothing for me before all this. In fact, I hiked a much steeper and longer trek with a giant tumour inside of me only a couple weeks before all this started. Anyways, I can assure you that I have never eaten my words, or a scoff, more. Twenty minutes would have been nice for the trek in; granted, in my defense, there was a steady incline the whole way there, since it took me probably closer to thirty to forty minutes with excessive amounts of stops to rest. Luckily, it was pretty much all downhill on the way back, which helped my time! It felt amazing when it was over, but it motivated me to keep working at getting my physical health back into some semblance of shape. I've taken it easy over the past couple days, but I am looking forward to getting back into a workout routine and challenging myself as much as I can.

I am awaiting my appointment with the oncologist next Monday. My appointment is via telehealth, which I am grateful for, as it means I don't have to travel to Vancouver. I am hoping that from this conversation I will know what the follow up plan will be, and what I can expect moving forward. It feels more like "hurry up and wait," but I suppose the next year of follow-ups will feel like that to one degree or another. Until then, I am going to focus on recovery and letting my body, and hopefully my poor brain, continue to heal.

1ST FOLLOW UP

APRIL 25, 2017

Yesterday was my first follow up with my oncologist. It was a good appointment, as far as cancer appointments go. I was anxious, and I realize that there was nothing to be anxious about in reality. I knew that the Doctor had no information for me, that it was a matter of me giving her information, but there is still this feeling of apprehension that comes with every appointment I have.

The appointment was via video, which I am grateful for, since travelling to Vancouver was not something I was looking forward to. My mom, Keith, and I attended. It was good to have them there for support, to be able to hear the information, and to also provide feedback about things that they see. My main issues right now are the continued tingling in my feet (which has moved from my toes to up my shin), my weight gain, and the chemo brain. It was reassuring to have her acknowledge these side effects and normalize them. Even though I've done my research, it's still nice to hear the doctor acknowledge those things. She encouraged me to be kind to myself and be patient with each of those side effects, which I find easier said than done. She also said that I should start to feel more my normal self over the next two to three weeks, which I am really looking forward to. Though I am feeling better each day, I still feel off.

The plan for follow up is part what I expected, and part not. As with any cancer, they look for symptoms more than anything else.

Ovarian cancer can be a challenge simply because the symptoms typically do not always scream *"cancer,"* but are usually misdiagnosed as other things such as IBS. I will have to pay attention to any bloating, hardness in my abdomen, weight loss, frequent urination, pain, changes to bowels, etc.... . Along with being aware of any concerning changes in my body, I will have a CT scan every three months, starting with a baseline one in the near future, as well as an exam and blood work. I expected the blood work and exam, but the multiple CT scans I wasn't expecting. I was initially told that they don't like to do scans with radioactive material very often as there are risks that come along with that; however, given my diagnosis, the oncologist said that she feels that the benefit of detecting any thing earlier outweighs the risks. I tend to agree. As stressful as those scans can be, I'd rather something concrete than the state of my body being based solely on my observations. So, for the first year, I will have follow-ups every three months, and then for the second year most likely every four months, and then every six months, etc.... . until hopefully five years clean, and then "cancer-free." Five years feels like a long ways away, so I'm going to focus on the next three months instead.

My goal for the near future is to get my strength, energy, and stamina back, as well as working on clearing the fog in my brain. This includes exercise both physical and mental, eating healthy, resting when needed, healing both physically, mentally, and emotionally, and just overall challenging myself to get back to my regular self.

WORLD OVARIAN CANCER DAY

MAY 8, 2017

Today is the first day that World Ovarian Cancer Day means any-thing to me. Up until September 2016, the idea that I could have cancer never crossed my mind, even though I was not unfamiliar with how unexpectedly and how unfairly the diagnosis of cancer could enter a person's life.

When my symptoms started, including fatigue, hardness in my abdomen, weight gain, increased urination (more than my normal, which is a lot on an average day), and feeling full quickly when eating, I knew something was wrong but couldn't quite put my finger on it. Eventually, I was also unable to comfortably lie on my stomach or on my back due to the pressure in my abdomen. I, like many in my generation, took to the internet to figure out what was wrong. When WebMD gave me my results based on my symptoms, ovarian cancer was on the list, but in the back of my mind I scoffed and figured I had a cyst of some sort. I admittedly Googled and used symptoms checkers for weeks, even when I had a doctor's appointment scheduled. I started to miss work or had to leave early, I slept for hours during the day on weekends, and I was struggling physically to do the things I enjoyed, including yoga, walking, and hiking. The thing that strikes me about ovarian cancer, and scares me still, is that there is no reliable screening test for it. This is why so many women are misdiagnosed, and why it takes so long to get a diagnosis that women often don't get diagnosed until late stages, which makes treatment and survival more complicated.

Awareness is so important when it comes to our health. As angry as I am with my body, which is something I continue to work on, a counsellor recently pointed out that while my body created "Felicia," it also gave me all the signs to do something about it, and luckily, I listened to it when I did. While I admittedly ignored those red flags for a little while, I was lucky enough to catch it at an early stage. As I have said in the past, it's important to know your body, and to trust it when it's trying to tell you something. And it's equally as important to speak up and advocate for your health whenever you are able. I think this is even more imperative when it comes to ovarian cancer, simply because the symptoms are often misdiagnosed as something else, such as IBS.

I am continuing to feel more myself. Keith and I were talking about our experience just the other day, and I said that it's amazing to me how I realize now just how unwell I was during chemo now that I'm feeling better. I look back on that time, and I try and have more compassion for my body and what it has been through. I still catch myself trying to rush my recovery, trying to workout almost every day and get back into doing the things I used to do, but I am also trying to not beat myself up when I can't do those things, or it takes me longer to do them. I feel better when I invest in my health, including watching what I am eating and exercising, but taking it easy and resting is also important. It also helps to have such amazing supports who aren't afraid to call me on it when I try and push things too much.

I am set up to do some blood work next week, my baseline CT the week after, and see my doctor at the Cancer Clinic here in town for an exam and the results of my testing early next month. Fingers crossed that things go as expected.

Returning to normal

May 17, 2017

It's been almost a month since the end of cycle six. Anyone who asks me how I am doing generally hears the same phrase, "I feel a little better every day," and while Keith refers to this as "the official line," it is still true. Aside from the fatigue, numbness in my feet, moderately poor memory and concentration, interrupted sleep and hormonal related things, I almost feel back to my "normal" self. I have been following the recommendations of my oncologist and the counsellor I spoke with and have been focusing on my self-care and recovery. I have been trying to get my brain, my mind, and my body back to a place I feel more confident in, and it's a slow process, but I feel good about it. I do brain games to help with the concentration, memory, word finding, etc... . I have been using meditations to help fall asleep when I need it, napping when I feel the fatigue is too much, and I have been watching what I eat and trying to get exercise every day. There was far more deconditioning in my body than I realized, so that part of recovery will take time. I'm not necessarily patient, but unfortunately these sorts of things cannot be rushed.

I had my blood work done on Monday. While there are a few low numbers, such as iron (as usual) and platelets, it's mostly good. The doctor has told me to increase my iron supplement, so I have started that, and hopefully that will help with my energy. The specific tests for cancer came back good, from what I can see.

I have access to my blood work results through My Health Portal (through Interior Health), and based on what I see, the numbers are good. While I am happy to see the numbers as they are, I am also cautiously optimistic (also as usual) because when I had the tumour the numbers were the same as they are now, so they aren't necessarily telling of what is happening in my body. I think I will feel more confident once I get the CT results and have a chance to speak with my doctor in June. Until then, I still am awaiting one more blood test result, and I have a twenty-four-hour urine screen to start tomorrow morning. Twenty-four hours of peeing into a cup and storing it in an orange container that looks like a gas can (but a gas can with acid/preservative) in the fridge. Oh, the fun things that come along with a cancer diagnosis! Ah well, just one new experience among many that cancer has brought into my life.

Hurry up and
Wait, Again ...

June 8, 2017

Today was my follow up with my doctor at the cancer clinic. It has been a long couple of weeks waiting for results of blood work, urine tests, and my baseline CT scan. I can't say that it has been an easy wait. I've ruminated on all the possibilities and stressed about the results each and every day, and with the exception of a few hours here and there, all day long. It's hard not to—it's not just test results, it's my life. I've been really focused on coping with the stress, and have kept up my working out 5/7 days a week, trying to eat healthier, talking to my supports, journaling, etc.... . I think I've done fairly well, with only a couple emotional crashes that I am able to pick myself up from fairly easily. Aside from the emotional side, physically I have been feeling good. I have a bit more energy each day, still requiring some downtime usually between 1:00–4:00 p.m., and I feel physically stronger. My feet are still suffering from the neuropathy, but hopefully that will go away soon (though the doctor said today that it can last six months to one year).

So, getting back to today. I knew the outcome of the CT late last week. I have access to imaging reports and blood work at home, so I was not surprised to hear the results today. I'm still on the fence about the effectiveness of accessing that information early. According to the CT report, there are "2 left retroperitoneal masses, suspicious for significant adenopathy" that were not present during my last CT or during my PET scan at the end of November. Essentially, I have swollen lymph nodes in my lower back area, and they are not sure if they are just swollen as lymph nodes can be, or if they are diseased. Thus, the hurry up and wait. I have been referred for a PET scan back at BC Cancer, and will have an appointment in four to six weeks. The outcome of that will obviously determine the treatment plan. If it is diseased, then we will most likely be referred back to the radiation oncologist in Kelowna and go from there. Other than that, my blood work and urine test were good, and the tumour markers came back negative. I'm a bit skeptical about these in general though, not to be a Negative Nelly, as they came back negative when I had the tumour still inside me. Remember: there is no actual test for ovarian cancer.

I'm feeling a bit overwhelmed, but also keeping my hopes up. There is a chance the lymph nodes are already no longer swollen, or that if there was disease in them it's already dead and they just haven't returned to their healthy size. We won't know, until we know.

It feels like a lot more of the same. A few steps forward, wait, wait, and wait some more, and then either a few more steps forward, or maybe even a couple backwards. Until then, I choose to try and stay as positive as I can and be hopeful that things will work out in my favour, and that I can continue to move forward in health. I'm grateful for all of the love and support in my life, and continue to appreciate and accept all good energy, prayers, and love. Keep your fingers crossed for me. Until later, we wait.

ANOTHER DAY, ANOTHER SCAN

JULY 1, 2017

Tomorrow is another big day in the cancer experience. I, along with my traveling supporters (Dad and Keith), are headed to Vancouver, bright and early for a PET scan—my second one, to be exact. After my CT results came back with those swollen lymph nodes, it was decided that we would look into what is going on in my body rather than "wait and see."

I have felt pretty confident these past couple weeks that it is for nothing, that we are going to be told next week (when I get the results) that it was all for naught and the lymph nodes are fine and there is "no evidence of disease." As it gets closer I feel like I've lost some of that confidence and every little ache or change to my body makes me feel a bit like I'm losing my mind. The fear of recurrence is around every corner, and sometimes it feels like a shadow I bring with me wherever I go. I've gotten very good at distracting myself, but it feels like this nagging voice in the back of my mind all the time.

I admit, I'm scared. I don't like to admit it, but really, what is the point in lying or hiding it? I think I'd have to be in a good amount of denial to not be. While I've been very lucky so far in terms of how my diagnosis and treatment have gone (obviously not lucky to be diagnosed with a rare ovarian cancer), this is real, and it sucks. These scans, while they have the potential to be reassuring, seem to drum up a lot of anxiety. The "what ifs" start to consume my mind. I try and think positive, and I know that if it comes back I will fight, but it's tiring just thinking about it.

I am ready for this scan to be over, and to have my results, and know what direction life is heading in. Until then, I feel a bit like a ship lost and adrift in the ocean.

Fingers crossed for me over the next few days; let's hope that the scan is clear and things can move forward.

P.s. Happy Canada Day (for tomorrow)!

IF EVER I WISHED
I HAD GOOD NEWS ...

JULY 5, 2017

It's a bit of a later post tonight; I wasn't sure I really wanted to write at all. I wish I had good news, but unfortunately wishes don't always come true. I had my appointment with my new oncologist (via video, as she's in Vancouver, and I am here in Kamloops). The appointment was to review my PET scan and make a plan from there.

Given I had never met this oncologist, I actually felt kind of bad for her; it's not easy to deliver bad news, especially via a video link, to a stranger and their support people. Keith and my mom were my people today, and I'm grateful they were there.

The cancer has "recurred," meaning my clean PET scan from November 29, 2016, did not last. I knew from the CT scan that I had two swollen lymph nodes, and learned today that I actually have four and that they showed "strong evidence" of disease. This implies that the cancer has moved, and this is not good news. They don't know for sure if it is the same cancer, and we are hoping it isn't. I know that sounds odd, but the type of cancer I had originally is rare and aggressive, and hard to treat, therefore we are hoping this is something else that would open more avenues of treatment.

I will have a biopsy of one the lymph nodes, most likely the one in my abdominal cavity, and it will be done in Vancouver in early to mid August. This will give us the information we need to know to determine what it is exactly that is in my lymph nodes, and what, if anything, we can do about it. It's another instance of hurry up and wait, and another instance of not having enough information to make a plan or to know where we go from here.

There is some good news, and that is that being young and being healthy are on my side, and the oncologist said this should give me more options down the road. I am not prepared to give up, and while I don't feel like the past few months have been much of a "fight," I am mentally preparing myself for that now.

The whole thing sucks. We discussed this earlier, Keith and I, and I am not sure there is a better word to describe it. I wish I had good news, and I wish that this was all over, but ovarian cancer is serious, and it is deadly, and that is why more funding and research needs to happen. If the biopsy comes back as the type I had before, I will be eligible for a research trial through BC Cancer Agency, and I am going to do that. There are no guarantees it will help, but it would give them more information into a rare type of cancer that could hopefully help others down the road.

Emotionally, I am all over the place. It's real, and I know it's real, but I still feel separated from the whole situation somehow. I've cried off and on all day, but as I said, I am preparing to fight with everything I have, and if the time comes that it's not enough, I will enjoy whatever time I have left with the people I love. We are a ways away from that, but it's obviously on my mind. I have a lot of life left in me, and I plan on enjoying it whether it's five years or fifty years.

BETTER HEAD SPACE

JULY 6, 2017

It's been a long day and a half, but I can honestly say that I feel more at peace with things, and actually feel the positivity that I have tried to maintain throughout this process. After some trouble falling asleep last night, I think the emotional weight helped me to sleep quite soundly. I woke up, and felt pretty nauseated, and said to Keith, "I was hoping it was a nightmare." Upon getting up, I decided to email my oncologist and essentially ask for more hope than I felt after our appointment yesterday. She promptly responded that she would call me later in the day and discuss it rather than risk miscommunication via email. With the help of my mom, I kept myself busy running errands and enjoying her company. We were able to talk about things, but I still felt unsettled.

The oncologist called this afternoon and I spoke with her alone. She delivered the same message, but I think I was in a better space to receive the information. While my cancer is labelled "incurable," it is still "treatable." I did not really realize the difference in these two concepts, but after some research and reflection, I feel more at peace with things. She clarified that if the biopsy (which she confirmed is a go, as the radiologist feels confident they can get a good sample) comes back as the mucinous ovarian cancer, it's difficult to treat, and while some people respond to treatment for periods of time, there is not a cure. However, this is more hope than I had yesterday. It means that there is a way to fight. I knew

I was going to fight, but wasn't sure how I was going to do that, given the way she put it yesterday. Today I feel reassured that no matter the outcome, they will have things to try, and even if they are not successful, I will have a chance, and that is all that I can ask for.

It's a rollercoaster of an experience; emotions are running high. I am choosing to cry when I need to, be angry when it comes up, and to try and just be grateful as much as I can. The support and love I have received since last night's blog has been amazing, and I don't think people realize how much it means to me. I have kept every card and note I have received since this started, and I go back and read those, along with the messages on Facebook and Instagram, and via text, on days when I feel alone. It is an important reminder that while I am fighting this, I have an amazing army behind me, and I could not do it without you all.

HOPE

JULY 11, 2017

I never realized how important hope is to people; and I suppose one does not think about it until they really need it. After last week I felt frantic, like my body was on fire with energy that I could not cope with. I felt sick to my stomach, I felt scared, and there was a feeling unlike anything I have every experienced. I have tried to describe it, but there are no words that do it justice.

I was at Keith's ball game on Sunday evening, and had a lovely time visiting with my parents (who also came to watch) and seeing some friends. People approached me and gave me their love, and while it felt great, I also felt sad. One interaction in particular came as a surprise to me. I was speaking with someone who has had personal experience with cancer, and they said to me "I have seen people with no hope, who were told there was nothing they could do come back from that," and I started to cry, but not tears of sadness, but tears of relief. I realized at that moment that what I had needed was not to be told "it'll be okay" from people who love me, but I needed hope from someone who had seen it first hand.

When I spoke with my oncologist, I was looking for that reassurance, and while she is a doctor, and deals with cancer all the time, she could not give me what I was looking for. I realize that this is not because there is no hope, but rather because we do not have enough information for her to comfortably say what I need her to say.

I realized from my interaction on Sunday that if I wanted hope, I needed to seek it out myself. I found a website called Inspire. com, and it has been extremely helpful. I joined the ovarian cancer community, and made a post asking for stories of women who had or have ovarian cancer, of various types, and were told they were "incurable" and managed/manage to live for years with treatment or without, etc.... . Essentially, I needed stories similar to my own that could give me some hope. I was not looking for false hope, as I am well aware of the prognosis for ovarian cancer. The result has been overwhelming and reassuring to say the least. The various women who have responded have had their own journeys, but they are all reassuring that it is possible to live with ovarian cancer. They don't minimize that it's complicated, and involves treatment, and plenty of ups and downs, but as one woman put it, "As long as you're alive, there is hope."

It's hard waiting, but I feel like I am putting as much of my energy towards the positive. I have changed my diet to cut out processed foods, in particular processed sugar, and increased my fruit and veggie intake, cut down carbohydrate intake, and I have started drinking at least three cups of green tea each day. I am also using essential oils, particularly frankincense and lavender, and have been meditating each day and using visualization. I am spending time with people I love, and who provide me with the reassurance, support, and at times reality checks that I need. I want to be able to say that I am doing everything I possibly can, and I think I am. Health is key, and I, like many, took it for granted for all my life. Even if nothing comes of the changes I have made, I realize that if age and current health are what are benefits to me, then I need to be the healthiest I can be.

I'm still scared, and I have yet to make it through a day without crying, but I am also incredibly aware of the happiness and love in my life. I want to live, so I'm going to fight for that, and for the people in my life, as hard as I can.

Personal power

JULY 20, 2017

I've debated about writing about my day the other day. It was not a good day for me, emotionally, but I realize that I started this blog to document my journey, and to not talk about those bad days would not be true to my experience.

The day started out okay; I felt a bit off emotionally already, so I took some "stress complex" from Nature's Fare, which has been helping me quite a bit. I stopped by my workplace to sign some paperwork, and felt good, and felt actually quite positive talking to people. It's almost that by reassuring them I can reassure myself. Then I headed to my doctor's appointment. I should preface this story by saying the few days prior I was feeling good, feeling hopeful, and life actually felt "normal," and I had made the two days prior without crying at all.

My appointment was not for anything specifically cancer related, but of course the conversation went there. The conversation cannot avoid going there when someone asks, "How are you doing?."

I was a bit teary, but said that physically I feel really good, but emotionally and mentally I'm on a bit of a rollercoaster, which is the truth. The conversation then led to the doctor reviewing the PET scan result, and from that moment on I was a ball of anxiety and stress. It's weird, because I know the results, I know the reality, but the way his tone changed, and the direction the conversation went was extremely upsetting. The doctor started to talk about how I should "get to work on my bucket list," and talked about having, "one, two, maybe five years." This led to a tailspin of anxiety and sadness and I left feeling, again, like I was dying the next day.

I called my mom and could not contain my fear and sadness. It's not that he said anything new, but it was as if my farewell tour had started with a good-bye from my family doctor. It was that same feeling I'd had when I left my last appointment with my oncologist—the most horrible of feelings, the Voldemort of feelings, the feeling that shall not be named.

I managed to pull myself together briefly to meet a friend for brunch. She was not aware of the seriousness of my situation, and while I tried to maintain my composure while in the restaurant, I'm not proud to admit that sitting there amongst the din of the busy restaurant, I shed tears—a lot of them. I realized that I needed to talk to someone—someone who could provide some reassurance and hope that I had suddenly lost.

I made my way up to the Cancer Clinic and tearily asked the receptionist if I could speak with the social worker or my cancer doctor (not my oncologist, but the one who follows me here). The social worker approached me, and I could not hold back my tears, and could not speak either. She walked me to her office, and I broke down on her couch. I told her, in what I am sure was a confusing explosion of words, what was wrong. I said that I felt as though there were conversations occurring and that I was not being told everything, and that I felt as though my medical team had thought, "ovarian cancer, well, we might as well give up."

The social worker was lovely, and calming, and looked into my file. She was reassuring in that she was looking at my file and said there was nothing written to indicate that they were not preparing to help me fight, and nothing to say that they had given up on me. There was the word "incurable," but not the word "palliative." She went and found my local cancer doctor who reiterated the reality of my situation, but also reassured me that there were still things to be done. She reminded me that I have a "low burden of disease," meaning that I do not have any symptoms, and that I am currently healthy, aside from the obvious issue with my lymph nodes. They also reminded me that "we still don't have all the information, and that the biopsy will hopefully give us the direction we need."

I left the appointment feeling better, but still frustrated with the medical approach. Sitting here typing, from a much better mental space, I realized that the doctors cannot give me the hope that I am truly looking for—not because there isn't any, but rather because they do not actually know. They don't have a crystal ball, they don't know how my body will react, but what's just as important, I think, is that they don't know me and what I am capable of.

I've been spending a bit of time thinking and reading about the universe, and one of the messages that I continue to come across is about personal power. What I have taken from these messages is that no one can take that power, and no one can take my inner strength, but that I am also responsible for not giving it away so easily. I feel that with my doctors I give it away freely, and that it leads to the distress I feel when I speak with them, which leads to emotional upheaval for days after I see them. I have the power to maintain my composure, and fight this fight the way I want to. It is, after all, my life I am fighting for.

I'm not in denial, but I'm also not giving up. I know that the reality is this disease will kill me, provided nothing else gets me first. I am not sad because I will die, because the reality is we all will. I just happen to know the most likely "how" of my death; the when is more of the mystery. I am sad because it takes something like this to really look at life and appreciate it. We all have an hourglass of sand, with life coursing through it, and we are never guaranteed more or less time than anyone else. I know we hear clichés about living life to the fullest, but I can honestly say it's true, that's why it's become such a cliché. We are not guaranteed a happy ending, we are not guaranteed long lives, we are not guaranteed love, peace, friendship, health, etc... . We have to work at those things, and maybe more importantly, we have to take the time to appreciate them when we do have them. I have a lot to live for, and no matter what the timeline is on that, I hope to live whatever time I am blessed to have to the fullest.

TRUSTING MY GUT

AUGUST 4, 2017

I felt like my old self again yesterday, the "pre-cancer Hayleigh." It was this blissful time when I didn't even think about having cancer, until I did. I have had more of these moments lately, and then something happens or a thought enters my head, and that "dark cloud" casts its shadow over whatever I'm thinking. I've had a lot more good days than bad, and for that I'm grateful. Waiting for this biopsy has been a challenge, but it has also been a gift. I've been better able to center myself, reinforce my positive attitude, and take care of myself physically, spiritually, mentally, and emotionally.

I keep telling those close to me that I have a gut feeling something good is going to happen. I'm not sure what it is, but I believe good news—whether it's about my health or not—is coming. And maybe that's a bit of denial, maybe that's a bit of wishful thinking, but something good is coming.

I know the situation is serious—as I have said before, I am painfully aware of that—but that doesn't change my outlook or what I believe to be true. One of my doctors told me, "It's okay to have negative thoughts. It isn't going to change the outcome." And while I understand where they are coming from, I also know that positivity and hope do make a difference. They can still tell me bad news, and remind me of "reality" all they want, and that will probably knock me of kilter for a few days (as it has done in the past),

144

but I know that I have to face this with the belief that something good will come of this; that no matter the outcome I, and more importantly, the people I love, will be okay, and that there is still a chance I can live a longer life than the statistics dole out.

For now, I'm doing better at living in the moment and shutting down the "what ifs" and worst-case scenarios. I'm meditating every morning and night, eating healthy, getting exercise, and spending time with people who fill up my soul when it feels lacking. I also remind myself that there is still hope, and as a friend recently said, "As long as you're alive, there is hope."

Every day I see something new in the news or online about ovarian cancer and treatment, screening, etc... . so you never know. Until then, I'll do what I need to do and what I can do, and hopefully my gut instinct will be proven right!

Pre-biopsy Jitters

August 9, 2018

Tomorrow evening we leave for the coast and make our way to Vancouver for the biopsy on Thursday morning. I received my "reminder call" today—as if I would forget something that has been very time-consuming in terms of cognitive space. I am both anxious, and yet still optimistic. Anxious, I think, mostly because it's a new procedure, I have to have a needle (or multiple needles in this case, which I don't exactly look forward to), and there are potentially life-altering outcomes—all of which are understandable reasons to be anxious. Despite these things, I'm trying to focus on the optimism. I've said to many people over the past couple weeks that I feel confident that there will be some good news coming my way, not just because of the laws of probability, but because I genuinely feel it in my gut. I don't know what it will be, but I feel like if you focus on the wins, no matter how small, it makes this journey a little bit easier. Plus, we've already been told bad news, that a) It's incurable; b) It's spread to my lymph nodes; and c) Depending on what type of cancer (unless it's something unexpected, which we cannot rule out in my weird case of rare cancers), they are both hard to treat. None of these outcomes will be a surprise.

I try and focus on today, and being in the moment (mindfulness), but it's hard not to spend a bit of time in the "what ifs." The reality is I do not have enough information to even know what exactly I'm worrying about anymore, and even Google and all of the support pages, etc.... . cannot give me the answers I am looking for. Therefore, I am choosing to be positive as much as I can. It's a bit easier to feel positive when physically I feel really good. I have been sleeping well, eating as healthy as I ever have, I have good energy (no need for naps here!), I have been able to get daily exercise, and I am symptom-free, as far as I can tell. I had blood work done earlier this week, in preparation for the biopsy and it shows general improvement since the end of chemo, with the exception of low iron (nothing new, even prior to cancer), and some still low platelets.

I am just ready for this waiting period to be over, and to be able to move forward, no matter the outcome. I have enjoyed this blissful period where the results can still be anything, but now I am ready to know the reality, and what it means moving forward. As of now, all that I know for sure is that I am alive, I feel good, I have so much love and support in my life and that no matter the outcome of this biopsy, I am still me.

So, fingers, toes, and what ever else you can cross for me that things go well on Thursday, and maybe one of these days, I will get to share some good news with you!

AND AGAIN, WE HURRY UP AND WAIT

AUGUST 11, 2017

This morning I got up early. I wanted to get myself centered before heading over to the hospital. It seems some days that managing my anxiety can be a full-time job, and I've found that taking some quiet time each day, and meditating has been really helpful. So that's how I started my morning, after a little cry with my mom. I can't pretend that I am strong all the time, but I find that once I let the tears out, I can move forward and recalibrate my brain to being positive and hopeful again.

The four of us made our way to the hospital and I had my blood work taken. Another win, as it only took one poke and was in my arm and not my hand! Once that was complete, we made our way to the CT department and waited for my turn.

A wonderful Irish doctor came to run down the procedure with Keith and I, and to have me sign the necessary paperwork. It was reassuring to have a nice doctor who made me feel comfortable and positive. Even when I called him a liar for how much the procedure hurt, I still liked him after it was all over. The next step was moving into the CT room and having my IV put in—two pokes, but at least they were in my arm, and didn't hurt that bad. The two staff, who I assume were nurses, were amazing. They made me feel comfortable and took my hand, squeezing like champs. Once the IV was in, I had to flip over to my stomach, as the biopsy was through my lower back. They had me move back and forth in the machine, finding the right spot for the biopsy. The doctor then put the local anaesthetic in, with a warning that it would burn, which it did. After it was "frozen," they continued to make sure that the aim was correct. This took a little while, and once the doctor was sure about it, he put in the needle in, and let me tell you, it hurt, *a lot*. I was not expecting the weird pressure/pain that happened, and they did not seem too concerned so I'm assuming they knew it was going to hurt. After multiple moves to get it in the right place, and multiple hand squeezes and almost crying, it was in. The POG team was present to get their samples, and it took a few "clicks" to get the samples they needed for diagnostics, and for the POG. Unfortunately, they weren't able to get all the samples in one spot, and had to move it slightly, which again was not in the least bit enjoyable, but luckily only involved one painful push of the needle. I was a bit worried, but luckily the doctor agreed that we needed to get enough in this biopsy because I definitely did not want to go through it again. A few more "clicks" and I was told the samples "look good," and that they got enough. I have probably never been so relieved for something to be over, and that includes the removal of a probably 15 lb tumour! They checked for any bleeding, put a little Band-Aid on, and after a few minutes of waiting, we were on our way.

Now we wait. Again. I am not anxious about the results, as I mentioned above, I think because once you've heard, "incurable cancer," "you'll need to consider your quality of life," "start working on your bucket list," etc... . it's hard to imagine feeling more terrified than those moments. I'm not saying that as a challenge to the Universe, but rather just from my experience so far. Even hearing "you have cancer" the first time was not as hard as that moment.

As much as treatments, procedures, diagnoses, appointments, prognosis, etc... . make this journey with cancer a struggle, it was spending time with people I love, today (and every day) that makes it manageable. Cancer, while it has taken a lot out of me emotionally, mentally, and physically, etc... . it has given me the ability to sit in those moments with my family, particularly today, when I got to meet the newest member of my amazing, support-ive, and growing family, and be grateful. And in gratitude is where I am going to try and sit until we get the results.

Here we go, again, and again, and again...

It has been a long few days. Longer than I could have imagined, and I've done my fair share of waiting since September of last year. I wish I could say I had great news, but mostly it's just plain old news. My oncologist called me this morning and let me know that the biopsy came back positive for the large cell neuroendocrine carcinoma (LCNET) of the ovary, which I had suspected all along. The good news in this, at least in the way I see it, is that the mucinous ovarian cancer was not in there with it.

The LCNET of the ovary is by no means great news, as it is just as rare and difficult to treat, even more so since I have already had the main treatment for it already. But (normally I hate the "but") there are still things we can try. As I am planning a trip in early September, which I am not ready or willing to not go on, I will have a CT scan upon returning in mid to late September and will again try the chemo combo that I was on previously. The doctor is comfortable with this, as I do not currently have any symptoms; therefore, there is no immediacy to starting the chemo again (for those of you who are wondering why on earth I'd be willing to wait). The rationale for trying the same chemotherapy is that they want to be sure it was not doing something to supress the tumour growth while I was on it, and now that there is a site to monitor, they can do that more effectively, a s it is unclear if the cells spread before, during, or after treatment. As the doctor said, there is no point in throwing out the cisplatin and the etoposide until we are 100% sure.

The other piece still in play is the POG. The samples were sent, and the oncologist said we might even have preliminary results by the time we get back from our adventure. I'm hopeful for this, as I still have faith the POG can be a game changer for me. I also inquired about a treatment they are bringing to BC (it's already running in Alberta, Ontario, Europe, etc... .) called radionuclide therapy (PRRT), which is for the treatment of neuroendocrine carcinomas. My oncologist initially said it's primarily used for the treatment of the pancreatic NETs, but also sounded curious and agreed to ask the team at BC Cancer about the possibility of it. If they say no, I am still going to advocate for myself, as having a primary ovarian neuroendocrine carcinoma is so rare that I'm sure someone, somewhere has to be interested in a challenge. I don't care if I have to go to Denmark for it—I want to try everything if there is a chance it could work!

So that is where we are. I am feeling surprisingly at peace. I think I knew there was a chance this was what it was, and to be honest, it is what I suspected. I am still keeping hope, and faith, that something good is coming my way.

But (again with the but, I know) I have other cancer-related news. As many of you know, my family has been through a lot this past year. My nephew was born very early at 1 lb 9 oz, and we almost lost my sister during that birth. Then I was diagnosed with cancer, and not "the kind you would want, if you have to have cancer." Then, my sister had to have surgery on her thyroid due to its massive growth, and the impact it was having on her body. We were kind of led to believe that all was good; she had it removed a few weeks ago, and was starting to feel better. Unfortunately, last night she, and we, found out that she actually has papillary thyroid cancer. It's curable and will involve removal of the rest of her thyroid in a few months, and then treatment with radioactive iodine, but things look good for her. It's incredibly stressful for her, for her husband, and of course our family, even with a really good prognosis. It makes you wonder, when is enough enough?! Luckily, she is strong, and we are here to support her, and we will get through it, like we do everything else: with a dark sense of humour, and love. Cancer has touched my family in so many ways, and to have three of us in our immediate family who have had to physically deal with it, it honestly feels unbelievable. It is just another reminder that life is so short and can change in an instant. So, if you get anything from this blog, it's to maybe hold your loved ones a little closer, and don't hold back in telling them you love them. Let go of the little things and remember what is actually important in life.

CRUISING ALONG ...

SEPTEMBER 7, 2017

It's been a while, but there hasn't been much to report as of late. I've been focused on enjoying life and living each day. It has been really nice, and while I've had a few moments of panic and sadness, I have been able to bring myself back to the present and remember that the present is all I can work with, the past has already happened, and no one knows what the future will bring.

I have been focused on being healthy, or as healthy as I can. We've continued to eat as clean and healthy as possible, and still feel the positive benefits of that. Keith and I went on a three-mile hike over the weekend, in place of my daily three-mile walks with my mom, and it was great. I felt strong, and the hike was much easier this year in comparison to last year, when I was already, unknowingly, carrying around a large tumour. I've lost a lot of the "steroid/chemo weight" and feel better about myself. I often hear, "you don't look sick," and it's important to remember that while there is cancer in my body it does not mean I am "sick." I actually feel better than I have in a long time, minus the backaches. Even my doctor said today, "Looking at you, it's hard to believe what the CT says ..." which is a nice compliment from a doctor who sees cancer patients all day.

As I mentioned, I had an appointment with my cancer doctor here in Kamloops (not my oncologist), and it was a good appointment. I actually felt good when I left, which anyone who knows me, knows that usually upon leaving I feel like I've been hit by an emotional freight train. I made the appointment, as I am concerned about my upcoming trip and this back pain. I don't know if the back pain is a symptom, but I suspect it's more a symptom of the stress, and the trauma of the biopsy, than of cancer.

My goal going in to the appointment was to stay confident, and not lose my "power" and my sense of hope. I also wanted to touch on the back pain, changing oncologists, and moving forward. My mom was my supporter today, and she was aware of the goals and was there to keep me strong. The back-pain stuff was quickly resolved, and she reviewed some reminders about travelling/flying when you have cancer. Then we moved on to the sensitive subject of asking for a different oncologist.

I have never been one to make waves, especially in a case when I am challenging an authority figure, so this was a tough one for me. It's not personal. Don't get me wrong, my oncologist gives me feelings of fear and dread (not her as a person, just in that she has had nothing but bad news for me since we met), but she is incredibly intelligent in her field, and is doing amazing work in cancer research, etc.... . The concern I have is that she is not a specialist in neuroendocrine cancer; she specializes in gynaecological cancer, and since the cells are no longer ovarian in nature, I want to be confident that the person directing my care is at the forefront of the type of cancer I have. It took a lot for me to bring this up, as I would hate to offend her, or any of the amazing doctors I work with, but the conclusion that I have come to is that this is my life. The outcome is life longevity vs. death, and I want to have the person who knows the best ways to manage this type of cancer, and hopefully one day (in my lifetime), cure it. Luckily my doctor here was incredibly supportive and understanding. She was not sure of the process, but she said that she would look into it for me.

Finally, we discussed moving forward, and this part was initially a scary part, but now I'm feeling more comfortable. I will have a baseline CT scan of my abdomen, pelvis, and chest when I get back to Kamloops. I will have blood work done and will hopefully speak with a surgeon's office to organize having a port placed shortly after I get back. Then, I will have what is called an octreotide scan, which will see if my tumours have the receptors that will allow me to be a candidate for the PRRT treatment. This is the part I'm super excited about. This technology is changing things for people with neuroendocrine cancer, and I just hope that I am one of those people! The scan can luckily be done here in Kamloops, so no travelling to Vancouver for that. Then we will look at chemotherapy again. The plan will be to start it at the end of the month; however, the outcome of the POG and octreotide scan may also affect that. So, while there are things to be done, there are still some things up in the air, but I'm actually okay with that. I feel like things are being done in the background, and it's oddly reassuring.

Anyways, sorry for the long blog today, but I'm feeling good about things, and wanted to share them with you. Fingers crossed that something, whether it's the POG, the PRRT, or the chemo, will make a difference. Getting ready for this fight!

THAT SILVER LINING IN ALL THE STORM

SEPTEMBER 21, 2017

I am home and have essentially hit the ground running. It was an amazing ten days, spent with new friends, Keith's family, and of course with the love of my life. It was nice to get away and feel less like there was a shadow following me. Instead, I felt free, and light, and happy, and, during an incredible sunset, which Keith and I watched from these beautiful red rocks with the Atlantic Ocean crashing against them, on September 12, 2017, I felt elated. Keith asked me to marry him, and I, of course, said *yes*!

Who Wore it Better?

Keith and I have been together since January 2016, and it was in our tenth month together that our journey with cancer began. As many of you know, I gave Keith "an out" on that fateful day, and he looked me in the eye and told me that he was not going anywhere. I've often struggled with guilt around the stress, anger, and fear this journey has brought into his life, and while I did not hesitate to say yes because I know that we are meant to be together (and knew this long before cancer was even on my radar), I also know that my life would not be half of what it is without him. Keith does not "complete" me, as I was already a whole person, but he does make me, and my life, better than I could have ever imagined. I am grateful for his companionship, his energy, his attitude, his sense of humour (no matter how weird and dark), his respect, and most of all, his unconditional love. He reminds me to live each day, and to stay in the present, while hoping for a future filled with as many years as I can get. He is an incredible person, and also incredibly humble, so he probably won't love this post, but as anyone who goes through cancer knows, the people who you have around you makes all the difference, and he makes me want to fight harder than I ever thought possible. Even if I get to live to 100 years old, or die at 120 jumping out of an airplane, it will not be enough time with him.

As much as I long to be back east, and away from every reminder of cancer, my life is here, and we must keep moving forward. As I mentioned, it has been hitting the ground running, and over the next two weeks life is filled with scans, appointments, etc... . Today I met with my surgeon for a consult to get my port put in. This will be the access point for chemo in the near future that basically puts a catheter into a large vein near my heart to allow the chemo to get into my body without damaging smaller veins. It has to be surgically implanted and will go under my skin near my left collarbone. You often don't see them because of how they are placed, and after all the trouble I had with the PICC line, I opted for the port instead. This will also allow me to swim, shower, bathe, etc.... . without issue. The surgery does not take long, but I will be put under (you can do with local anaesthetic, but after my last experience, I want to be knocked out!). It's day surgery, and it will take place on October 3, 2017, the one-year anniversary of this whole experience starting. Prior to that surgery, I will have my O-scan over the course of two to three days next week, and a CT scan on the 2nd of October. So, it's a bit of a hectic schedule of cancer-related appointments, but at least we are doing something now.

I am feeling good, mentally, physically, emotionally, and spiritually. I still feel positive that something good is going to happen, and that somehow, some day, I will get good news. I continue to have pain, but again, I am not sure what the cause is. I am back on track with eating healthy (vacation is over for that!) and will get back on track with my daily walks tomorrow. While I still feel sadness and fear, I also feel hopeful and happy. One of the things I have learned through this experience is that life is what you make it. I have had to let go of what I thought my life would look like and try and embrace it for what it is. I have so many things to look forward to, people to spend time with and love, and cancer cannot take that from me, unless I let it.

PEI Engagement

Happy "Cancerversary"!

Life happens in an instant—or at least, that's what some people say. I don't disagree with the sentiment. One year ago, October 3, 2016, I left work in the morning to see my family doctor, for an appointment I had scheduled a month earlier to investigate a hardness in my abdomen. Along with that hardness, I was feeling extremely fatigued—not just tired, but truly fatigued (trust me, there is a big difference), I was peeing every ten minutes, I had no appetite, and when I did eat I was full after a couple bites, and I had gained about 15 lb in the month prior. Little did I know, but that appointment, that day, one year ago, changed my life in a way I never imagined possible. Most people consider the day they were diagnosed with cancer their "cancerversary," but I consider October 3 to be that day. It was the day that everything changed, and it was the day that the mass, which would turn out to be two types of cancer, was "found."

It's not a day you'd think I'd want to celebrate, and it's not so much a celebration as a remembrance that I have survived the past year, a year that many women with my diagnoses do not survive. Mucinous ovarian cancer and large cell neuroendocrine carcinoma of the ovary are two extremely rare forms of cancer and are often not diagnosed until it is too late. I was "lucky" in the sense that they were caught earlier on, but as you know, that does not guarantee an easy journey and does not guarantee remission.

This past year, I've learned more about life, pain, facing mortality, depression, anxiety, sadness, and fear than I ever thought possible, but I've also learned more about support, joy, silver linings, strength, unconditional love, hope, gratitude, and blessings than I could have ever imagined.

Cancer is a scary word, and I think that I was naive at first. I figured we'd found it early, we removed it, we figured out what it was, we treated it, and that I could get back to life. I was terribly wrong. My body, the universe, whatever entity is out there, all had a different idea.

Cancer is my full-time job these days, but it does not define me the way it did at the beginning. It's something I go through every day, but it is not who I am. It has taught me to let go of the little things, to have hope, to see the bigger picture, and to recognize what is actually important.

I've been blessed through my first year of this journey with the love and support of so many people. Love and support that I believe has helped me to survive this past year. Family who have gone above and beyond, friends who let me talk about my fears even though it scares them or saddens them, a fiancée who has been my everything and has created safety for me to go through this journey however I need to in each moment, and so many other supports who have reached out with a phone call, a text, a message on Facebook or Instagram, a card, etc.... . I've found support from strangers I've met online, survivors who give me hope, and support groups that have given me guidance. So, thank you to each and every one of you for caring enough to follow my updates and ramblings, and know that I love you all.

The next year won't be any easier, and I'm trying to focus on each step as it comes, and not get too far ahead of myself. Tomorrow, my "cancerversary," I will have my port put in during day surgery, and it will mark a new chapter in my journey. I'm hopeful that something will work, and I feel in my gut that something good will come of these various treatments we are looking at. I am continuing to do everything that I can to thrive in this experience, and to fight for my life, however long I am blessed to have.

JUST CHECKING IN

Surgery was yesterday morning, and everything went well. I now have my very own port embedded just under my left collarbone. I won't lie—it hurts. More than the PICC surgery, but I truly feel that at the end of the day it is the better choice for future treatment. My only real complaint, which I plan to take up with my doctor, is that they cut you open, feed a catheter into your heart, and attach this device under your skin, sew you up, and then send you home—all without anything for pain! Honestly, it's bloody inhumane. I felt that way about the PICC insertion, but this is definitely more. Luckily, I had leftover pain medication, but needless to say, it's been a long couple of days even with that. Put it this way, you almost got a rambling blog post at 1:00 a.m. this morning while I was lying on my couch not able to sleep, but I reigned it in. I overdid it this morning, but rested this afternoon.

Tomorrow I meet with my doctor here in Kamloops. I'm nervous, though I'm not sure why. I'm not sure what the appointment is about, possibly giving me an appointment to start chemo, maybe to give me scan results, but as anyone with a health issue knows, doctors' appointments cause a lot of anxiety! I'm reminding myself that it doesn't matter, that results don't matter, I'm still me, and no matter what the outcome of the scans, I will move forward and live my life the only way I can. But fingers crossed for me, just in case!

Thanksgiving

October 7, 2017

It's been a long, slightly hectic, and overly emotional week. As you know, Monday I had a CT, Tuesday I had my port put in, Thursday I met with my doctor at the cancer clinic here in Kamloops, and by Friday I started chemo again. As with anything in health care, as much as we want things to move quickly, when it moves that quickly, it's never a good sign.

My CT came back with spread of the tumours, including some small ones (less than 2 cm) in my lungs, more lymph nodes in my chest, and one on my pancreas. It was not a complete surprise, as we had not been doing any form of medical intervention, just life-style changes. While the lifestyle stuff is important, and makes me feel healthier, the medical stuff plays such an important role. It was a whirlwind of an appointment, and honestly, I don't remember much, though Keith took notes (which I can't bring myself to look at just yet). The ultimate outcome was to start chemotherapy again as soon as possible, to hopefully "get a lid" on any more growth and/or spread. Again, chemotherapy was not a surprise, as we had discussed it previously, but I was not expecting it to happen the next day.

For the next month and a bit, I will have three days of chemo, with eighteen days off, the same pattern as last time. This time will be with a different, but just as strong chemo drug called carbo-platin, with etoposide, which I had last time. This cycle, because it started so quickly will include one day of IV meds (which was yesterday) and two days of oral etoposide, which I will take today and tomorrow. Then, at the end of the month, I will have three days of both of the meds via IV. It looks like we will then do a CT to see if there is any effectiveness, which I am holding out hope for good results from.

Yesterday was a tough day for me. I was up early after not having slept well for the past few nights and made Keith and I breakfast. I threw up a couple times, I think out of nerves, but managed to get myself together. I went for my usual walk with my mom (two miles instead of three, though) and came home to try and mentally process as much as I could, which involved some good crying, and some attempts at meditation, and some pre-chemo meds. I usually need a couple days to regain my confidence, and process things, and to get back my positive outlook, so having chemo scheduled in there made things a bit more difficult.

I feel like every time I have an appointment it throws me off balance, and it feels like every ounce of hope that I cling to gets taken away piece by piece, until I can somehow put it back together again. It's probably the hardest piece of having cancer. Hope, as I've said, is everything, and I remind myself that we wouldn't be going through chemo, and we wouldn't be looking at PRRT in Edmonton if there wasn't still a chance, and though I slowly feel those dwindling as we move forward, I still hold on to them to give me more time. It's a double-edged sword, wanting to move forward but also being afraid of what's around the corner. I'm tired of bad news ... but still have that feeling that something good is coming. I follow a lot of different people through social media, and their stories remind me that even for those who had brief times of NED (no evidence of disease), they had to go through times like this, times of bad news, and multiple rounds of chemo, and multiple surgeries, trials, etc... . So, maybe someday that can be me.

Emotionally, I'm getting stronger, back to where I was last week. All of the love and support I have received gives me strength, from all the lovely messages on Facebook and Instagram, to the flowers, cards, texts, and the beautiful gestures, like yesterday, when one of my best friends met me before chemo to lend me her essential oil necklace filled with "peace and calm" to help me get through the day, that make this journey that much easier.

Hayles and Keith Dance (((One of our favourite stress relievers))).
Photo credit to Natalie Dollman Photography

Physically, I'm healing a little each day from the surgery. I got to use my port for the first time, and though I think it was the source of a lot of my anxiety, it worked like a hot damn! The nurse seemed a bit nervous, given it's still a bit swollen and bruised, that it might hurt, but honestly, other than her looking for the right spot, I didn't feel a thing. It worked very well and reaffirmed that it was the right choice. I'm tired, which is not uncommon with chemo, but also due to poor sleep for the past few days. I have been up at around 3:00 a.m. each morning, but I force myself to stay in bed until 5–5:30. Plus, this morning I woke up hungry (could be the steroids), but I needed to take my pre-med and the oral chemo on an empty stomach, so I figured I better get up, take those, and then I could eat sooner rather than later!

This weekend is Thanksgiving, and I have so much to be thankful for this year. To start, I am thankful for each and every day I have on this earth. I am grateful for the amazing support in my life. From my mom, who through her own process of this journey, is still the strongest, most incredible person I know. She cries with me, but then gives me the kick in the butt I need to be confident and feel strong. For my dad, who's quiet strength and belief in taking things as they come reminds me to stay present. My sister, who though she is going through her own cancer battle, checks in with me and makes sure that I smile each day with silly pictures or Facetime with my amazing nephew. Keith, who is my everything, who is a lighthouse in this storm, and who holds and protects my heart and soul. I'm incredibly grateful for all of my family, who go above and beyond, and who love me unconditionally. My friends, who offer to take me to chemo, or send me flowers to brighten my day, who forgive me when I flake on plans because I'm not up to it but send me messages of love throughout the day. And all the people who support me in all the ways that make me feel so much love. I'm also grateful for my incredible and constant (sometimes too constant) companion, Liam, who doesn't even let me go to the bathroom without his supervision or take a bath without him keeping me company.

In a world where it is so easy to get drawn down into the drama, sadness, and fury of what is happening out there, I am choosing to be grateful, and to recognize that no matter what each day brings, I have so much to be thankful for. Love to you all, and I wish you all a Happy Thanksgiving filled with happiness, love, and good food.

P.s. What better time to be back on steroids than Thanksgiving, am I right?! Bring on the turkey!

HOLY HEARTBURN!

OCTOBER 12, 2017

I've settled back into living life with cancer after what felt like a punch in the gut from last week. I still struggle with not feeling hopeless at times, and I feel like I still need to find a way to experience my doctor's appointments, etc... . without losing my strength and hope, but it's not an easy task. They speak in terms of "statistics" and other cases, and what they "know" and in my case what they don't know, and while it may seem like I'm in denial, the reality truly is that no one knows exactly how this journey of mine is going to play out.

The chemo this time has been a slightly different experience. As I mentioned, because we started chemo as soon as possible, I had one day of IV carboplatin and etoposide and two days of oral etoposide. I initially liked the idea of oral medication, simply because it meant a few less hours in the chair at the cancer ward, hooked up to an IV, but honestly my stomach might not be able to handle two to three cycles of oral medications, which it doesn't have to, as I will have IV meds next time. The chemo schedule for the two days of oral was pre-meds, then an hour before I could eat (or two to three hours after), I would take the etoposide. Overall, the nausea and stomach upset were different compared to the IV meds of my first round—I'd say more intense in the moment, and more concentrated, but seemed to pass earlier. I am on less anti-nauseant medications, including steroids, this time, but I'm actually okay with that. So far, no eats! I have been able to manage the side effects, without any real issue, except maybe this brutal heartburn. I have had the worst heartburn, which I did have the first round, when I was on cisplatin, but holy moly, I have had three days of terrible heartburn. Enough, that I have had to sleep sitting slightly inclined for the past three days. But, if the chemo is doing it's job, it'll all be worth it.

Overall, I know that the chemo experience is not over, and that the side effects come along the way, but as with everything, we just take it as it comes.

Round Two: Cycle One Done

November 6, 2017

It's been a long few weeks, and I'm not even sure when I last wrote. Things have settled a bit with the chemo. My first cycle of round two was quite difficult, much more than my first rounds were, but I survived. Cycle two started last week and while I did not tolerate the chemo as well as I have in the past, I again made it through. I am really hopeful that the chemo is working. I know it won't cure anything, but to have it work well enough to stop, slow, or shrink the cancer would be amazing.

Mentally, I have struggled at times over the past few days. I try and stay positive, but this sense of panic sets in at times where it's difficult to get my brain out of that place. I think the added mix of hormones is not helping the situation. Luckily, I have been able to get myself out of these ruts. I think it probably has to do mostly with the CT scan I have scheduled this Friday. The scan will give us an idea if the chemo is working, and given my history of bad scans, my anxiety is high. As I've said before, "scanxiety" is a real thing, and it's rearing its ugly head lately. I have found some comfort in connecting with other women who have ovarian cancer, and people with high-grade neuroendocrine carcinoma. Often it can be a double-edged sword, as you often see messages of people who have passed or are not doing well, but I find that the stories of the women who have survived—those who have been on chemo for years, or they have made it into NED (no evidence of disease)—give me a bit more hope when it is lacking.

I've also been slowly working on my will. I have never done one before, so I'm not sure if everyone who does one feels sad when they do it. I'm assuming most people do get reflective and probably a bit depressed when doing a will, given that it forces you to look at your life and mortality. It's an important thing to have, and even if I was not going through this journey I would, or at least should, be doing one. It just makes you think more about the people and the things you leave behind, and I feel like I think about this more than necessary already.

Anyways, that's where things are currently; we are hanging in there. Just praying that the chemo is doing its job, allowing my body to rest and heal, and being grateful for this life.

COMING UP ON THE
END OF CYCLE TWO

NOVEMBER 17, 2017

It's been a long couple weeks, and to be honest, I have not had the energy to even plug in my computer, let alone type anything.

Cycle two has been much the same as cycle one. I have struggled with nausea, vomiting, aches and pains, fatigue, and light-headedness. I run out of gas very quickly these days. I am doing my best to rest and take it easy, but it's still frustrating for me to not be able to do all the things I want to do at any given moment. Also, my hair has just started to fall out over the past few days, so I may be getting a haircut sooner rather than later, but I'm hoping that because my hair came back so thick that falling out won't necessarily mean going completely bald again.

I know that at my last check-in I mentioned doing a CT scan, but that afternoon I actually spoke with my medical doctor with a specialty in oncology (MDSO) here in Kamloops and my oncologist in Vancouver. After speaking with my MDSO, I asked to do one more cycle before we check, just to be sure to give the chemo the best chance to show if it's working or not, and she agreed. Most research I've read has said two to three cycles is the best to see effectiveness, so three cycles it is, with a CT scan booked for the beginning of December. I am hoping that the chemo is at the very least preventing any growth or spreading, though shrinkage of the tumours would be the best news.

After I spoke with her, I got a call from my oncologist, and actually felt more hope than I have in awhile. Unfortunately, I did not get approved for Quebec's PRRT trial, due to my tumour "not fitting their criteria." However, after speaking with the team there, my oncologist was apparently informed of a couple other neuroendocrine trials, including an immunotherapy trial in Toronto, that I might be eligible for. She also noted that we cannot wait longer than the third cycle to do a CT scan, so that if it's not working we can "change directions," which gave me a bit more hope that there is a direction to change to—something I had not believed was an option. For the first time in a while I felt hopeful and like I have a chance to really fight; even if nothing comes of the trials, it's been nice having that hope.

So, that's where we are. Getting through each day as best as I can, and being grateful for all the love and support I receive on a daily basis. Cycle three starts on Monday, so wish me good luck getting through that. The MDSO prescribed me another medication to prevent nausea, which will hopefully help me get through next week, and then it's letting the chemo and my body do what they need to do to hopefully be fighting this fight.

P.s. My sister had her surgery to have the rest of her thyroid removed yesterday, so if you can, say a little prayer or send good energy for her that she comes through it well and gets good news that she is cancer-free!

I HUGGED MY DOCTOR TODAY

NOVEMBER 22, 2017

It's been a long week—well, in reality, it's been a long year and a bit–but after throwing up 5/6 days, needing a blood transfusion, and having a surprise head CT today, this week has felt longer than usual.

I got sick last week and summed it up to anxiety/anticipatory vomiting. My blood work came back, and my haemoglobin was 78 (normal is 118–151) but everything else looked okay. This resulted in a blood transfusion that included one unit of blood and fluids each on Monday and Tuesday. Therefore, chemo was pushed back a week. I felt amazing after the first transfusion, but that was short-lived. During my second transfusion I got sick twice, which had my doctor concerned, not because I was having a reaction to the blood, but because I was still throwing up.

On Monday, in an effort to figure out the vomiting, I had an X-ray to see if there was a blockage, and was told no blockage (yay!) but also that even though you can not compare accurately an X-ray and a CT scan, it "appeared" that the lymph nodes in my chest were either the same size or possibly a little smaller. I told the doctor I'm taking it as a win, and believing they are smaller! Then, after more vomiting, including twice during my blood transfusion yesterday, the doctor called me and said that even without any other symptoms and just to be cautious she would like to order a head CT if the vomiting didn't stop.

She called today, and though I was feeling somewhat better, I have continued to throw up, so she wanted me to get the scan done. I was admittedly terrified. Scanxiety went from 0 to 100 during that call, and I told her I was scared to know if it had spread to my brain. I suggested that since Keith is also sick (though not vomiting), it might just be a flu, which she agreed with, but said "Let's do it anyway, and deal with whatever the scan comes back with after." So, given the time crunch, both of us feeling sick, exhausted, and fatigued, we got tidied up (a.k.a., out of pyjamas), put on our medical masks, and headed to the hospital.

My head felt as messed up as my body, and my brain was a scary place to be for those couple hours. The CT went by smoothly, quick IV and quick scan and we were directed up to my doctor on the eighth floor. We waited patiently, me thinking worst-case scenarios and Keith, all congested, trying to bring me back to the present. Every time we saw my doctor walk, by I think we both stopped breathing. She started walking towards us, and for the first time ever I got two thumbs up and a big smile. I walked towards her and gave her a huge hug. She said, "It came back normal." No brain mets for me! Even though I still have cancer in my body, it's not spread to my brain! I said, "That's the second time you've given me good news in one week!" Which I had told her she would get to give me one day!

And we met in the exam room briefly. Obviously, there is still concern about why I am vomiting so much, but it's not coming from my brain, and that is the best thing I could have heard today. We're hopeful it's the flu and passes quickly, but chemo can tend to prolong symptoms of things like colds and flus.

Anyways, we are home and both resting, as the physical and mental toll of our outing today was more than we needed today. It's strange, because though my body feels horrible, I'm so happy.

It's a small victory, but it's a victory, and I'll take it! I couldn't wait to share with all of you, and hopefully I'll have more good news to share as we move forward! Next CT will be to check the efficacy of the chemo next Friday, so fingers crossed for more good news!

FOURS DAYS IN ONE BLOG

DECEMBER 2, 2017

Be prepared, this is a long one, as I have plenty to share, and I'm finally able to sit down and process some of this past week, which, as many of you know, has been an incredibly long one.

After about a week and a half of vomiting, fatigue, mild nausea, and no appetite, and as I noted in my last blog, an X-ray to look for blockages and a head CT scan to look for possible brain metastases (a.k.a., mets), I ended up not being able to get out of bed on Saturday. This prompted my request to go to the hospital for fluids on Sunday morning. At this point, I was still under the assumption I had the stomach flu, so left Keith at home disinfecting everything and asked my dad to take me to "just get some fluids and be home in the afternoon." Both were, of course, amazing and agreeable, so my dad and I set off. Luckily—and anyone who's ever been to the Kamloops ER (or really, any ER) knows it's lucky—I was able to get into the streaming ER within fifteen minutes. We waited a little while to see the doctor, but in the meantime, we got my port accessed for easy fluid provision and blood work and started that process. I met with the ER physician, and he was good with the fluids but acknowledged that more investigation needed to be done to find out the cause. My rational brain knew this was going to happen, but the naive, put-my-head-in-the-sand part of myself really hoped they would not bother.

So, another abdominal X-ray and eventually an abdominal and pelvic CT later, they confirmed my worst fears. The chemo was not working, and unfortunately the cancer had spread. In particular, the tumour on my pancreas appears to be the main culprit, but it has spread to other lymph nodes in my abdomen and in my lungs. From what they see, it appears that the pancreas tumour is pushing into my lower stomach, but also my duodenum, which has created a smaller opening that large or solid foods cannot seem to make it through. It was devastating to hear that, truly, but I think my dad, Keith, and I were so numb at that point that it did not really phase us, and maybe to some degree it hasn't fully hit us still. The other complication that they found were some small blood clots and what they called "tumour clots," which apparently is quite common in cancer patients. So, based on that information, we knew I would not be going home after "a couple of hours of fluids."

My dad and I stayed in the ER that night, thanks to the amazing nurses who I know from the past working in the ER who set us up in a private room for the night. And though we got barely any sleep due to the lively crew that was coming and going from the ER that night, it was nice to have a bit of privacy and space to try and process what we had learned. It was great to have my dad there, and I am blessed he was here this week, and even though I kept insisting he go home, and go back to work, he was there every step of the way. Keith was sent home, by me, even though I know it was hard for him, but no sense in all three us trying to get comfortable in the hospital-supplied furniture!

The next morning (Monday), I was moved to a great, relatively private, but extremely hot, corner room with a view on the fourth floor. Monday was a flurry of doctors and specialists reviewing information and connecting with my usual cancer team to discuss plans. These were the conversations I feared the most, but luckily, they were more reassuring than upsetting. Don't get me wrong, my dad had to remind me to breathe on multiple occasions, but between him and all of my supports near and far I made it through the day. My doctor from the cancer clinic in Kamloops came up to see me and reviewed a bit more about the outcome of the results and set me up with a chest CT to confirm that there are more "nodules" in my lungs. She was in contact with my oncologist in Vancouver and they had decided to present me to the tumour board again to see what these amazing minds could come up with to give us a bit of hope, and hopefully a tool or two we can use to try and fight this aggressive monster. I met with an internal medicine specialist who focused on managing my symptoms, particularly the nausea and vomiting, pain, and blood clots. Pain and blood clots were relatively easy to manage; I was given pain medication, which we have been working on setting up for steady coverage, and blood thinners to hopefully deal with the clots. The rest of my time was spent napping and visiting with family and a couple friends that popped by. The days, though you would think felt like eons, actually went by quickly.

Monday night Keith stayed with me, and Dad went home to get an actual night's sleep and take care of Liam. Unfortunately for Keith, it was probably my worst night in there. Until that evening I had been on a steady infusion of anti-nausea medications, but they decided to try and "push" the meds into my port via a syringe; however, that resulted in throwing up within one to ten minutes, depending on how fast they administered it. So, every couple hours, without fail, the nurse would come in quietly, push the medication, and leave, and Keith would have to assist me in promptly throwing up. I almost think at one point he was still asleep and just reacted instinctively from his fold-out chair/bed, rubbing my back, reassuring me I was okay, and removing the evidence of my still unmanaged stomach issues.

Tuesday, the changing of the guard, as I liked to call it, happened with Dad arriving within minutes of Keith leaving for work. I'm not sure how he navigated even making it to work, but he was a trooper. Tuesday, I believe was spent resting, hearing new plans, and waiting on potential plans. It all feels like a blur, but again, between medications, exhaustion, and stress, the day flew by. We met with a dietician who discussed the possibilities of an NG feeding tube and maybe even a feed port in my abdomen. This was upsetting, but I understood where they were coming from. Since I had arrived, I was being sustained on broth, jello, ginger ale, and water: a diet I am still pretty much following until I am comfortable testing what I can actually eat without being sick. Ultimately, my doctor in Kamloops did not feel we are at a place where we need to discuss that, as I am still able to get nutrients into my body, just not necessarily enough. We were all relieved at her feedback. The day previous, I had learned that my mom had changed her flight and would be home to help take care of me and would arrive on Tuesday night. I find most mom's just have a way of making things better with their mere presence, especially when you are sick, and mine is no exception. I was happy for her to be coming home, and even maybe a little more happy that the plan was for me to go home, with new medications as well as learning how to make and administer my own IV medications.

As many people know, and people who have spent time in hospitals know very well, plans have a way of falling through. Wednesday morning, I had the chest CT and blood work done first thing. My blood work came back, and my haemoglobin was back to the high 70s. This meant another blood transfusion, which of course, did not even start until around 4:00 p.m., and it is a long slow infusion. Given the time I needed to receive the blood, and confirm my haemoglobin was back in check, and trying to learn how to set up my home IV plans, I was told I would not be going home until the next day. I was surprisingly good with that news, because I was still feeling dreadful and wanted to be confident in being well enough that I would not have to turn around and come straight back to the hospital. My mom was my faithful companion that night, changing roles with Keith, so he could get some actual sleep in. Even though it was one of the most painful nights due to abdominal bloating and pain, the likes of which I have never experienced before, my mom rubbed my back, and grounded me in the present in a place of more hope and positivity.

In terms of what we learned on Wednesday, it was confirmed that there were more lung mets and we learned a little more about my weird and aggressive tumours. Apparently, the POG (Personalized Onco-Genomics) trial had come up with one interesting piece and that is that my tumour, while ovarian in it's original form, had mutated and was "acting like a gastrointestinal (GI) tumour," and so instead of re-presenting me to the gynae-cological board, they spoke with the GI tumour board who gave a suggestion of trying a chemo that is used to slow progression, but possibly treat, GI tumours. I love that they are willing to think outside of the box, and it makes me a more hopeful that they aren't giving up on me just yet. They also were considering trying radia-tion, which was eventually nixed. There are still some possibilities of trials, but the doctors have said that this will be unlikely due to timelines. The cancer grew and spread in two months more than it had in the few months prior, and trials take time—time that definitely without chemo I do not have, and often you have to stop chemotherapy if you want to be eligible.

Today was also when the word "palliative" started getting used more fluidly. It's a bit of a kick in the stomach, to say the least, but as I have said in the past, it does not mean I'm imminently dying, but it is moving towards that process, and being prepared in terms of paperwork, and also mentally and emotionally for when that day comes. To be clear, they have not given me a "timeline," just recognizing that the aggressive nature of my cancer makes time that much more precious.

Thursday morning, I felt like a new woman, despite the still-bloated abdomen, and a new back and hip pain from sleeping in the hospital for four nights. I got up, and my dad, who had stayed with me overnight, went for a brief walk to try and stretch and get things moving better. I was desperate to leave, and luckily after final training, and organizing prescriptions and plans I was set free. It was a long day, and the back pain definitely was not helping my mood or my ability to rest, but I am so glad to be home, and with Liam and Keith, and in my own bed! I set up my eight bags of anti-nausea meds for my rigorous schedule of home IVs, organized my new, and many, oral meds and blood thinner injections, and tried to rest as much as I could.

This brings us to today—I know, *finally!* I hardly slept last night because of the pain, and the schedule of meds including a midnight and 3:00 a.m. IV infusion. I "woke up" exhausted and anxious for my first round of the new chemotherapy called irinotecan. Between medications, IVs, and puttering around the house this morning (using a burst of energy I was lucky to have), time passed quickly and my parents took me to chemo. I slept on the car ride there, slept through most of the chemo infusion, and slept all the way home. I unfortunately did have a reaction to this new medication; however, this is apparently quite common and resulted in a shot of something in my arm after throwing up, and I fell back asleep almost instantly. I made my way home, ate lunch (soup, not just broth!), made up the bags for the next twenty-four hours, and hung out with my auntie until Keith got home. This afternoon, and it could be the steroid talking, I felt more myself than I have in a long time.

So, wow, that was a lot of information, which I apologize for, but I like to document it not only for sharing my journey with all of you, but also for my own recollection. This experience has always been overwhelming, and this blog gives me an opportunity to share what is happening and how I am feeling. It has been a struggle to try and understand how I am not more upset, but honestly, I think after everything that has happened, you do become emotionally numb to words/phrases like "incurable," "metastasis," "disease progression" and "palliative." I still feel like I have life to live, and while each day takes me closer to an outcome yet to be determined (as is all of our cases), I plan to live those days to the best of my ability. I again want to say that I am so grateful for all the words and gestures of love and support from people; thank you for keeping my spirit up, and for giving me strength and motivation to fight, which gets more difficult when you feel like I had been feeling. Sometimes all it takes is someone to say "keep fighting," or for someone to take the time out of their life to visit to talk about anything but cancer, or to be an extra eyes and ears when learning how to make home IVs. I am again beyond blessed, so thank you.

Bringing in thirty-two

December 14, 2017

It's been a long (and kind of weird) few days. I won't go too far back, because it feels like a lot has happened since I last wrote, but I will say that since coming home from the hospital a couple weeks ago, life has continued to throw me both ups and downs.

In some ways, life has stabilized; for example, I am now on a continuous infusion of Gravol to manage the nausea, and basically curb all the vomiting (with a few exceptions). I carry a handy little bag that my sister has dubbed "Doris," which connects to my port and provides me with 24/7 medications. While carrying Doris can be a bit of a pain in the butt, she allows me freedom, she allows me to eat and has given my body some semblance of feeling normal. After almost three weeks of vomiting, it's a small price to pay, especially since I can be home and not in the hospital. It's amazing the technology that is available, and I am most grateful to have added the home IV team to my health care team.

No, since having the nausea and vomiting basically under control, my body has decided to change things up and give me some pain to muddle through. Over the past three days I've started to experience some fairly intense and challenging-to-manage pain, to the point that my medications were not working. I could not sit comfortably except to lie over the arm of my couch in an awkward leaning/hunched position, and as a result, I ended up spending yesterday in the ER. Not the way I planned to ring in my

32nd birthday, but to be honest. the relief of pain even for a short time was worth the six hours there.

After another night of not sleeping, I woke up on Tuesday, called the cancer clinic to see if I could see my doctor, and hopefully avoid a trip to the ER. Unfortunately, I was not that lucky, and was directed to the ER, so I called my mom, and asked her to take me. Hoping that maybe it was something manageable like a kidney infection, etc.... (I know it's weird to wish for such things, but when the alternative is your cancer is spreading/growing, a kidney infection sounds pretty good), we made our way to the hospital. My luck did turn for the better, for a short time, as I was triaged and in the back within fifteen minutes. They did the usual urine screen, blood work, and what is normal for me, a CT scan, and eventually some wonderful pain medication. It turns out my kidneys are A-Okay, which in terms of the bigger picture is great, but it still left me with pain that they are not quite sure what it is. It seems that the mass on my pancreas has grown slightly in the past two weeks, so we are going under the assumption that it is the mass pressing on something causing me to walk like a bald Quasimodo. It took six hours to figure this out, but again it was six hours of pain relief, so I cannot really complain. They gave me some new pain medications and sent me on my way home. Not the ideal way to spend a birthday, but it was at least somewhat relaxing; I got to hang with my mom, and had a nice dinner at the local pub before heading home to bed.

The pain-free feeling lasted only so long, and by the time I was ready for bed, I was hurting. The struggle I find with taking all of these different (and new) medications and managing symptoms is I often wait and see, because I second-guess what I should be doing. I do not want to fall into the trap of taking too much, but also realize it's futile to be in pain, as it does not serve me or the people around me. So, waking up after about an hour of sleep in terrible pain, I probably should have considered going back to the hospital, but in my stubborn nature I persevered and ended up in and out of pain and trying to balance that with the direction of taking one to two tablets of pain medications every four hours when I needed it every two. After spending the night on the couch, trying to get comfortable, watching PVR'd cooking shows and cheesy romantic Christmas movies, I decided this morning that I needed to do something, and as it would happen, the Universe seemed to be listening.

I got a call from my home health nurse noting that she had seen I was in the hospital yesterday and inquiring as to how I was managing the pain. I explained that I simply was not managing it, despite my best efforts to listen to the directions of the ER doctor and use all the tools of pain management I could muster. This is when she offered hospice.

I've talked in the past about the power of language and the struggles I have with terms like "incurable" and "palliative," but "hospice" hit like a shot to the chest. My immediate reaction was "No, I don't need hospice," but the somehow still-functioning part of my brain that has struggled with pain for the past three days said, "Whoa there, Hayleigh, listen to what the woman has to say." She informed me that as part of the palliative program, there is the ability to come to hospice and work with the doctor to get pain/symptom management support in a 24/7 setting, and with support and direction. I could hardly say no given how bad things had gotten, and I agreed. Then came probably one of the hardest cancer journey phone calls I've had to make: my mom. I knew what the word "hospice" did to me; I was horrified at what it would feel like for her to hear the words, "Mom, can you take me to hospice?"

So, after getting help to get dressed and packed for a couple nights, and a good angry/sad cry, mom and I embarked to the hospice house. It's hard to explain the disconnection that happens in your head and your heart when going to a place like hospice but being relatively vibrant and feeling good with the exception of the pain, but it's was a very surreal experience.

I am almost glad to be coming into this current situation, as I know I am going home in the end, and I can process things easier knowing that I am going home after a couple days, once the pain is under control. I have already made the decision that when the time comes I would like to pass at hospice, and knowing that made coming here scary, but being mindful and knowing that I am not near that time in my journey helped me to work through this experience.

Today was spent resting and getting a sense of what my body needs to manage the pain. The staff, and the ability to get help for my pain, has been amazing. Given my birthday was kind of a bust yesterday, my mom arranged with the staff here to have a little impromptu birthday dinner (the traditional birthday meatloaf celebration—much to my poor mother's embarrassment) and she made up a delicious meatloaf dinner, which we shared as a little group in the hospice kitchen area. It was not the normal birthday, but it was still a perfect moment with family, comfort food and love.

Today was yet another reminder of how blessed I am to have the people in my life, particularly my mom. I cannot say enough about the strength and love my mom has; there are no words that could aptly describe how incredible she truly is. Her day starts with driving her daughter to hospice, and consists of helping me settle in, running around getting new bags of Gravol for Doris, picking up things from home to make me more comfortable, grocery shopping to make me a delicious birthday dinner, stopping by again just to have a visit, cancelling appointments for me, informing people of what's happening, arranging appointments, and these are only the tip of the iceberg of her day. She never complains, she just does, and does, and does. If ever there was a Wonder Woman, her name is Holly, or as I like to call her, Mama-Bear.

Hayles and Cheriese

Well, I think that is it for me for tonight, as the lack of sleep for the past three nights, and the pain medication, are catching up with me. Thank you again for all the birthday love and wishes, and I ask that if you haven't done so recently, maybe send some extra love to the amazing mom, moms, or mom-like figure in your life. Until later, goodnight.

Hayles and Mommabear

Hayleigh Noel O'Brien (née Connell)

Hayleigh Noel O'Brien (née Connell) was a young woman with a zest for life. She was a beloved daughter, sister, auntie, and wife-to-be. Hayleigh lived in Kamloops, BC, with her partner, Keith O'Brien, and her dog, Liam. She worked as a mental health clinician, helping adults with addiction and mental health challenges. She loved to travel, having visited England, France, and Egypt. Hayleigh was diagnosed with mucinous ovarian cancer with large cell neuroendocrine carcinoma shortly before her 31st birthday. During this time, she documented her experiences while continuing to look to the future, planning her wedding and various travel plans. After a courageous battle, she passed away on December 16th, 2017.

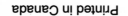
Printed in Canada